WHAT TO DO WHEN YOU ARE DEAD

LIVING BETTER IN
THE AFTERLIFE

CRAIG HAMILTON-PARKER

STERLING ETHOS

An imprint of Sterling Publishing Co., Inc.

New York / London
www.sterlingpublishing.com

DEDICATION:

To all you who fear death.
May this work help you to realize that life,
once given, can never be taken away.

STERLING and the distinctive Sterling logo are registered trademarks of Sterling Publishing Co., Inc.

Library of Congress Cataloging-in-Publication Data
Hamilton-Parker, Craig.
 What to do when you are dead : living better in the afterlife / Craig Hamilton-Parker.
 p. cm.
 Originally published: c2001. With no illustrations.
 Includes bibliographical references (p.   ) and index.
 ISBN 978-1-4027-7660-1
 1. Future life. I. Title.
 BL535.H36 2010
 133.901'3--dc22

                                                        2010018991

10 9 8 7 6 5 4 3 2 1

This 2010 edition published by Sterling Publishing Co., Inc.
387 Park Avenue South, New York, NY 10016
Originally published in 2001 by Sterling Publishing Co., Inc.
© 2001 by Craig Hamilton-Parker
Distributed in Canada by Sterling Publishing
^{c}/o Canadian Manda Group, 165 Dufferin Street
Toronto, Ontario, Canada M6K 3H6
Distributed in the United Kingdom by GMC Distribution Services
Castle Place, 166 High Street, Lewes, East Sussex, England BN7 1XU
Distributed in Australia by Capricorn Link (Australia) Pty. Ltd.
P.O. Box 704, Windsor, NSW 2756, Australia

Manufactured in the United States of America
All rights reserved

Sterling ISBN 978-1-4027-7660-1

For information about custom editions, special sales, premium and corporate purchases, please contact Sterling Special Sales Department at 800-805-5489 or specialsales@sterlingpublishing.com.

"Death is nothing at all. I have only slipped away into the next room. I am I and you are you. Whatever we were to each other, that we are still.

Call me by my old familiar name; speak to me in the easy way which you always used; put no difference in your tone; wear no forced air of solemnity or sorrow; laugh, as we always laughed at the little jokes we enjoyed together; pray, smile, think of me, pray for me; let my name be ever the household word that it always was; let it be spoken without effect, without the trace of a shadow on it.

Life means all that it ever meant; it is the same as it ever was; there is unbroken continuity. Why should I be out of mind because I am out of sight? I am waiting for you, for an interval, somewhere very near—Just around the corner. All is well."

—Henry Scott Holland

CONTENTS

INTRODUCTION

THERE IS ANOTHER SHORE BEYOND the horizon of physical life. It is not a "great unknown," as it has been visited by many spiritual travelers from our world. On their return, they have related strange stories that fill us with awe, much as did the tales of explorers when they first traveled the seas to Australia or the Americas. Some have journeyed to this place during sleep, while critically ill, or under hypnosis. Others have traveled there during meditation or a mediumistic trance, or by using techniques that enable the soul to travel outside the physical body.

Believers in this "other shore" usually live better lives. Even if some do not profess it philosophically, they may still have the feeling that that shore exists. A voice deep within tells them it is the truth. A person who believes in or, even better, has actually experienced the afterlife has a completely different outlook on this life to that of the materialist. Knowledge of a next world brings with it a strong sense of personal responsibility and morality. A person who knows there's an afterlife realizes that the immortal human spirit is here for a greater purpose than just accumulating possessions, status, fame, or power. In contrast, those with no belief in an afterlife tend to create a society fixated on short-term results, without much thought for the consequences of their actions. To the believer in an afterlife, it is apparent that life is an opportunity to grow by enhancing the soul's capacity to give and receive love. Life gives us the chance to change ourselves and to understand the purpose of existence. Those who acknowledge the world of the spirit are more likely to take personal responsibility for their lives and live to a higher moral standard than those who don't.

Could it be that the problems of our time are a result of our forgetting the knowledge of the afterlife? Would we still have the urge to accumulate earthly things or to strip the world's resources for short-term profits if we knew for certain that we would pass this way again? Supposing we knew, as fact, that every action we take will affect our future and come back to us like a cosmic boomerang. Would we then be so keen to cause others pain or plot for selfish gain?

What a utopia we could enjoy if the majority of people here and now recognized that we are only the temporary custodians of this world. Even our human bodies are made from the dust of stars that burned out millennia ago. Dust to dust to dust. No, the transitory things of the world cannot give long-term support. They will all pass away, even the giant sequoia and the deepest ocean. But the things of the material world are as nothing compared to the everlasting spirit. Its pristine light is our true reality.

Many people live out their lives avoiding the dark thoughts of death. It is simply too frightening to contemplate. Death shatters everything. Up to the very last moment, most people refuse to face death. When my father, for example, was diagnosed as terminally ill with bone cancer, nobody in the family would even mention the word *death* to him. My father steadfastly refused to accept that he would soon die and fought a tragic battle to the end. It brought to my mind the words of the poet Dylan Thomas: "Do not go gentle into that good night, / Old age should burn and rave at close of day; / Rage, rage against the dying of the light."

If we lose someone close to us, it brings thoughts of our own mortality. "When our parents die, we know that we're in the next wave," said a friend my age. "It brings home the fact that death comes to us all." Nonetheless, if we examine our innermost feelings, we may admit to an innate "knowing" that there is something else after death. A voice, a whisper, somewhere deep inside, says, "Don't worry about death. Everything will be all right."

I am fortunate in that I know that little inner voice is right. I have amassed too much evidence to believe otherwise.

WHAT TO DO WHEN YOU ARE DEAD

"It's Life, Jim, but not as we know it."
—LEONARD NIMOY (AS MR. SPOCK, *Star Trek*)

◦◦◦

ONE FOOT IN HEAVEN

I am a mental medium. The adjective "mental" distinguishes those mediums who bring messages from the next world from those who produce physical phenomena such as voices, lights, levitation, or the manifestation of ectoplasmic figures. A mental medium's job is to provide verifiable evidence of human survival after death through information from the spirit world. Some of this information reveals what life is like in the afterlife. The material received from spirit communicators via mental mediumship is the cornerstone of this book.

A medium must always strive for accuracy and not give vague statements that could apply to just about anyone. Plenty of people spout psychobabble, but much of it can be quickly recognized as foolish fantasy. A good medium will always strive to provide clear and verifiable detail. Only if the mediumship is good can we trust that the information given about the afterlife deriving from it is also accurate. What you will read here is not fantasy or material simply arising from the unconscious. It has come during mediumship from spirits who have proven their identity to the sitters. Also included is information derived from yogis, metaphysical thinkers, and mediums of the past.

MEDIUMISTIC COMMUNICATION

Spirit communication happens when the conditions are right. On this side, there needs to be a cheerful atmosphere of expectation. Once this is established, the medium is usually able to blend thoughts with those being projected by the other world's spirit communicator. These thoughts are perceived by the medium as a voice, pictures, or sensations. By putting the various impressions together, enough evidence can be established to prove that contact has been made with a discarnate loved one. The energy that fuels this wonderful phenomenon is the power of love. It is love that builds the bridge between the two worlds.

Often, evidence for life after death is strong enough to reassure the converted, but not conclusive enough to convince unbelievers. It is much more difficult to work with a skeptical person. I have given very accurate evidence, when demonstrating in the supportive atmosphere of the Spiritualist churches, but to provide the same detail to a hard-nosed journalist is another matter. Nonetheless, I have endeavored to demonstrate mediumship on television, over the radio, and in front of skeptics. Sometimes I fall flat on my face, but as a rule I have managed to provide clear evidence of survival, even when working in the most hostile of conditions.

When Amanda Ward came to see me, I had no idea that she was a journalist who had been commissioned to write a scathing article about mediums. This was to go into the international woman's magazine *Marie Claire* and the *Daily Express*, a top British newspaper. Her assignment was to visit five mediums. She was to give them no information about deaths in the family, nor were any of them to know that she was researching a story. I learned later that I was the last on Amanda Ward's list of mediums to see. On meeting her, she was polite enough but had a guarded manner and was very suspicious of me. I knew this was not going to be an easy consultation. The title of her exposé, which appeared some weeks later, was "Are All Mediums Frauds?"

Relating to me, it began, "I chose Craig Hamilton-Parker after accessing his website www.psychics.co.uk. According to Craig, his wife Jane, his daughter, and even his dog are psychic. He has written several books on the subject and charges £50 [about $100] for an hour's sitting, but warns me he has to spend twenty minutes 'tuning in' before our meeting at an old school hall near Southampton. I wait on a tatty sofa while Craig prepares himself.

"We sit at the front of the hall surrounded by rows of chairs, with children's collages hanging on the walls. It's early evening, the sky is darkening and it's eerily silent. I'm a little scared. 'You've got a really lovely aura,' he begins. 'It's blue, which means you'd be good at healing.' I'm flattered and relax slightly. I have given him no details, so what he says next makes the hairs on the back of my neck stand on end. 'I've got a lady here. I'm getting a pain in my chest and finding it quite hard to breathe. The illness was very quick, unexpected,' he says. 'I'm getting the date of 11th November. And is the date 28 February important? Is this your mum's mum, or someone on your mum's side?' I think, it's my mum—she died on 21 November [near enough] and 28 February was my parents' wedding anniversary.

"Craig continues, 'She was good at organizing. She's telling me that her favorite flowers are daffodils and that she's one of seven. She loved swimming, especially when she was older, and that you changed your job around the time she was ill.' He's just described my mother's character, her favorite flower, the correct number of siblings, and her main hobby. He was spot on about the job, too. I went freelance a few weeks before her death.

"He carries on, 'Is there a newborn baby here? It's either yours or a sister.' I confirm that it is my sister. He continues, 'She wouldn't have lived long. She doesn't look like you, but she's grown-up now and has long ringlets.' We were non-identical. I feel totally freaked but strangely pleased that she is now an adult.

"Craig does ask if my father is alive. When I tell him no, he says, 'He had bright blue eyes with a mischievous twinkle.' Yup, that's Dad, and I want to hear more. Craig looks at me decisively, 'He had a very short name. Three letters. Don or Ron?' Oh, my God. Dad was called Stephen Ronald, but everyone knew him as Ron. 'He had a very selective ear where the women in the family were concerned. He used to joke about your mother being "the battleaxe" or something,' says Craig. Attila, actually, but what the heck. 'And he used to torment you, but in a nice way,' he says.

"Next, I ask the impossible—what was my father's pet name? Craig closes his eyes and goes silent. 'Is it something to do with eating?' he asks finally. Craig is making a chewing action with his mouth. 'I'm getting sweetness. It's definitely fruit. Is it cherry?' As a child, I loved pineapple chunks and used to call my father 'Chunks.' Craig may not have got it exactly, but it was damn close.

"I'm overjoyed. To me this is proof that my father is there, somewhere. How else could Craig have known those things? But what's unnerved me most is that Craig has adopted my father's mannerisms—stroking the top of his head, and pinching the brow of his nose as he's been talking. In fact, for one strange moment in the dim light, I almost believe it's my dad sitting there. I leave feeling buoyant and comforted. I find myself talking to my parents in my head. Thanks to Craig, I'm convinced they can hear me."

Amanda Ward came to me a skeptic and left with tears in her eyes. It is fortunate that I gave a comparatively good reading and sad that her report was scathing of the other four mediums in her article. My media work over the years has taught me how to overcome the barrier of "armored" people.

I hope that relating this case here provides some basis in demonstrating that the communications I receive from the spirit world are valid and that the material I am presenting about the afterlife is derived from true mediumship. Another of my books, *The Psychic Casebook,* gives further testimonials about my work as a medium, and detailed case histories are published on my website at www.psychics.co.uk.

YOU ARE NOT THE BODY

"The body and the soul! The body was born and will die.
But for the soul there is no death. It is like the betel nut.
When the nut is ripe it does not stick to the shell.
But when it is green it is difficult to separate from the shell.
After realizing God, one does not identify anymore with the body.
Then one knows the body and the soul are two different things."
—Ramakrishna

How much time do you spend trying to satisfy the needs of the physical body? You may enjoy good food, sex, a nice and spacious home, regular vacations, or a big car. You may draw comfort by surrounding yourself with luxury or by wearing the most expensive jewelry. We live on an endless treadmill, moving from desire to desire. It's like eating a tasty meal; we enjoy it, but sooner or later we get hungry again.

I'm not saying that you should wear a horsehair shirt and retire to the forest. It would be inappropriate to stop eating or to throw away your material possessions and pleasures. All of these things are good, but they are also transient. They do not last. Desire is a trap, and that applies to the physical plane, the astral plane, and the causal plane.

The Buddha said that the cause of all suffering is desire (attachment). Liberation from the endless cycle of birth and death comes when you can let go of all attachment and desire. People who worship material things usually fear death the most. The thought that the physical body will one day perish fills them with utter dread. Have you ever met a beautiful woman, such as a top model, who is just getting to the point where her looks are changing? Instead of allowing an inner beauty to develop and shine through, she busies herself in a frantic attempt to maintain her external beauty. Yet we've all been touched at times by people so spiritually beautiful that we never noticed whether they were physically beautiful or not.

The truth is that we are not the body, yet we spend all of our time pampering it. In the developed world's cultural climate, we carry with us a heavier burden of material thinking than any generation in the history of mankind. The result is that we've forgotten that the physical body is only one small part of our being.

DEATH DENIAL

In earlier times, the fear of dying was used by religion to undermine individualistic thinking and to increase our dependence on the church. A fear of an eternal hell and retribution kept the heretics in check and society in control. It was the perfect way to hold on to power and maintain the status quo. Religion, in its worst form, is a notorious system of mind control that uses the fear of death to manipulate its victims. It achieves the very opposite of what its saviors, saints, and sages taught.

Sadly, death is still taboo. A history of spiritual corruption has meant that most people do not see death as a blissful transcendence. Instead, we are encouraged to cling to the material and avoid all talk of death—particularly when death creeps close. Everyone knows that you are dying, yet your relatives can only talk about banal things such as the weather. Nobody dares to talk to you about your oncoming trip to the unknown. Added to this lonely predicament, you may have to endure the dispassionate world of intensive care. There is an almost hysterical desire to keep life going at all costs, even if it means keeping you alive for a few more days of suffering.

Would it not be better if, instead of existing in a state of denial about death, we were to consider embracing it when it approaches? Clearly this is easier said than done, but to consider the possibility of a life beyond death and to think about our own mortality will help us to realize that death can be a mystical experience that need not fill us with fear and dread.

The realization that our soul consciousness goes on after we've died is a call to use our lives wisely. It is a call for us to wake up, and to put to good use this wonderful opportunity of living on planet Earth. Fortunately for us, the physical body is not the sum total of our being: we also have a spiritual body, a body of light that will transport our consciousness into the next stage of existence.

THE BODY OF LIGHT

"People shouldn't worship my bones . . . we reside in our bodies and then we move on."

—ALBERT EINSTEIN

EVERYTHING THAT EXISTS is energy in motion. The only difference between soul and body, consciousness and matter is the rate of vibration. Only the Absolute—God in Primal State—does not vibrate and is at perfect peace. When God stirred, the universe was born.

The motion of energy at the time of what is known as Creation first manifested as cosmic light and cosmic sound. The vibration of this conscious energy became progressively more gross until it metamorphosed into the material world. The afterlife, which is a level of reality that vibrates at a higher rate to the material plane, therefore existed before the material universe. Similarly, consciousness and the life force itself are the vibration of energy at different frequencies.

Indian mysticism calls the life force that animates matter *prana.* (The Chinese call this same energy *chi.*) It is the missing link between consciousness and matter. Prana is finer than atomic energy and permeates everything. It is the substance of the heavenly worlds and the life principle of the earthly world. Prana takes two forms: the cosmic vibratory energy that is omnipresent in the universe, structuring and sustaining all things, and the specific aura that sustains each human body or life form.

In short you, and I, are made of both matter and prana—body and spirit. I am further blessed to be able to see prana.

Ever since I was about six years old, I noticed shimmering

lights around people's heads. As a child, I had no idea what caused this effect. In fact, I simply assumed that everyone saw it too. In some questioning of adults, however, I was met with reactions of surprise and disbelief. Over the years since, however, I have learned to trust that special vision that I have.

I now know that the lights I saw then, and still see, are what mystics call the *aura*. You may also be able to see or sense it; for example, you may notice a "shining" around a person's head, or get a "feeling" of someone's mood. It might help to think of it as a tenuous "atmosphere" surrounding the human body—just as the planet Earth has an atmosphere. The aura is an energy field—it's our individual life force.

Recognition of the fact that humans are surrounded by an aura dates back millennia. Christian saints are, of course, traditionally shown with a halo around the head. The Ancient Egyptians did the same when portraying their gods or important human beings, as did the Hindus, Buddhists, Greeks, and Romans. These expressions of belief continue to the present. The aura is generally recognized as having seven layers. Most psychics see only the first three—those closest to the physical body. The outer auric layers are concerned with the soul and spirit, whereas the inner auric layers relate to mind, emotions, and health.

The aura, shaped like a symmetrical egg of fibrous light, surrounds the whole of the body. To some, it resembles a heat haze that radiates from the person, but shimmers with light and energy. It contains every color imaginable, including those beyond the visible spectrum. Or, as Sir Winston Churchill put it, "I expect orange and vermilion will be the darkest and dullest colors and beyond them will be a whole range of wonderful new colors which will delight the celestial eye."

During the 1930s, the famous American psychic visionary Edgar Cayce was able to give startlingly accurate medical diagnoses based upon the colors and information he perceived in the auras of his patients while he was in the astral state. Cayce, while in trance, could even see such emanations at a distance, over many miles. A perceptive psychic will notice various colors in the aura that indicate a person's state of mind and physical health. Students in my workshops, which have included nurses and doctors, report being able to sense hot or cold spots, and some have even learned to see and feel the "black spots," or gaps, within another person's auric structure.

The aura is in a constant state of flux, reaching out and pulling in depending on how we relate and react to the world. The color of the aura also changes constantly with every emotional experience and thought. There may be a dominant color that stays with the person throughout life, but many of the colors change from day to day.

WHAT HAPPENS TO THE AURA WHEN YOU ARE DEAD?

When a person is ill, the colors of the aura go dark and pull in close to the body. When death comes, the aura withdraws into the body, ready to leave in what mystics call the *astral body.* This astral form of the human body is made of prana and looks as if it is made of light. There are three main sheaths that encase the soul.

The Physical Body

The physical body houses the spirit. It is a wonderful piece of organic machinery but is not the real you. The body is like a set of clothes. We put it on when we are born and cast it aside when we die.

The physical body is animated by the prana life force of the astral body. It is connected at seven main points, called the *chakras* in Sanskrit—which translates literally as "wheel," although most people envision them as lotus flowers of light. The seven major chakras, or energy centers, correspond to the endocrine glands of the body and run upward along the spinal chord.

Centered along the spine, the chakra points correspond with the base of the spine, just below the navel, just below the rib cage, the center of the chest, the top of the throat, the center of the forehead, and the very top of the head. As a person spiritually awakens, the life force becomes centered on the upper chakras. A person who is interested mainly in sex and power, for example, will have the prana energy centered on the chakra at the base of the spine. A person focused on spirituality and enlightenment will have the prana energy centered on the crown chakra at the top of the head.

The Astral Body

When I see the aura, I am looking at the outer part of the astral body. The Hindus call the astral body the *Linga-Sharira*, a Sanskrit word meaning "design body." The Ancient Egyptians called it the *Ka*, the Greeks called it the *pneuma*, and the Jewish Kabbalistic doctrines call the astral bodies the *five souls*. Other terms include the *etheric double, perispirit, doppelganger, phantom, spook,* and so on.

The astral body is an energy equivalent of the physical body. It has astral duplicates of all the internal organs, the nerves, the arteries, as well as the physical frame and even our familiar face. According to the Theosophists, this astral body also has a record of all the human memories experienced by the person. All living things, including plants, have an astral framework that is with us from birth and determines the growth and form of the physical being.

The part of the astral body that reacts with the physical body is sometimes called the *etheric field.* This can be seen by psychic people as a blue/red light that runs like a line around the body frame. It is most easily seen at the tips of the fingers, if you look at them in a very low light. A technique I teach my students is to look between the gap that's formed if you hold your two index fingers close together. In subdued light you may see fine lines of light dancing between the two fingers. This is the etheric field of the astral body.

The astral body is also considered the seat of the emotions, so it is sometimes called the *emotional* or *desire body*. Some people also call the higher function of the astral body the *mental body*. Other esoteric teachings refer to a number of distinct planes of the afterlife, each with its own corresponding "vehicle" of consciousness. Just as there are seven chakras, so too are there seven etheric sheaths that vibrate at different levels of spirituality.

The Causal Body

According to Indian mysticism the human being consists of three main bodies: the physical and astral bodies, and a second spirit body called the causal body. The three body sheaths are the different vehicles of our consciousness. They clothe the inner being. The astral body has the same form as the physical body but is made up of subtle matter (prana). The causal body, which psychics can see as the aura in the form of an egg, is the body of light. This is known as the *intelligence and bliss sheath*.

The three bodies roughly correspond to what we would call *body, mind, and soul*. Furthermore, each of the three bodies conforms to a state of consciousness. The physical body functions in the waking state, the astral body in the dream state, and the causal body in the deep sleep state. The inner self that is housed by these sheaths exists in the fourth state of consciousness, which is the ever-wakeful state of pure awareness.

Only the causal body endures over many incarnations, whereas the physical and astral bodies are formed anew at each new birth. The causal body is the repository for all our karmic impulses. The yogis tell us that the causal body can alter reality, create worlds, and bring about materialization. However, even this body is not eternal. When a person attains full God, it too is dissolved into the infinite spirit.

For simplicity, I will call, in the pages that follow, the astral and causal bodies and their parts "the body of light."

WHAT GURUS DO WHEN THEY ARE DEAD

When death comes, we discard the first sheath—the physical body. The body of light then exits via one of the chakras.

The chakras are like doorways. When we were preparing to be born, we entered the body of the baby form that our mother was growing. According to my spirit guide, who talks to my group during trance, this happens at the time of the "quickening," when the new individual begins to stir in the womb. Your spirit entered via one of the chakra points. Which chakra you chose to enter by depended upon how spiritually evolved you were. If your soul state was still on the animalistic level, or this is an early incarnation for you, you would enter through one of the lower chakras. If, however, you had spent many past lives in the quest for spirituality, you would enter through one of the higher chakras. This entry determines your motivations and life goals. Fortunately every person also has the opportunity in life to develop his or her spirituality. When this happens, the prana rises gradually to the higher chakras.

At death, the body of light leaves through the highest chakra to which it can attain. In India, the eyes of a corpse are checked to see if they are looking upward toward the head. If so, it means that the departing spirit has exited via the crown center at the top of the head. When this happens, it is said that the spirit has attained enlightenment and immediately enters the highest heavenly state.

According to the Hindu yogic teachings of the *Prashna Upanishad,* the chakra through which the spirit leaves the body determines the course of its journey after death. The prana life force moves up the central subtle nerve channel in the spine and carries the spirit to its appropriate chakra doorway.

The spirit of a person who has spent his or her life in the pursuit of God consciousness passes out of the body through the crown chakra (known as the *brahmarandhra* or *vidriti*). Exiting the body through this chakra is said to be extremely hard to accomplish, as the slightest hint of earthly desires will block the doorway. Departure through this chakra has been likened to trying to pass a thread through a very fine needle. It will jam if even one fiber of desire is sticking out.

Even the great gurus can flinch at the thought of death. Paramahansa Yogananda was one of the first great Hindu teachers to visit the West, and he founded in 1920 the Self-Realization Fellowship in Los Angeles. His own guru was Sri Yukteswar. On approaching his eighty-first birthday, Sri Yukteswar made the announcement that he would soon die. Suddenly, this great guru looked visibly upset, but he soon regained his composure and remained in a blissful state throughout his death passage. Yogananda said: "For a few moments, he trembled like a frightened child." Yogananda then quoted the words of another great guru: "Attachment to bodily resistance, springing up on its own nature, is present in slight degree even in the great saints."

Three months later, Yogananda was staying at the Regent Hotel in Bombay. At three o'clock in the afternoon of June 19,

1936, the spirit of Sri Yukteswar appeared in Yogananda's room. Yogananda's spontaneous reaction was to embrace his old guru. To his amazement he was hugging a real body. "Yes this is a real flesh-and-blood body," explained Sri Yukteswar. "Though I see it as ethereal, to your sight it is physical. From the cosmic atoms I created an entirely new body . . . I am in truth resurrected—not on earth but on the astral planet. Its inhabitants are better able than earthly humanity to meet my lofty standards. There you and your exalted loved ones shall someday come to be with me."

His guru then told Yogananda all about the heavenly worlds, and gives us a few clues about what enlightened souls do when they are dead. "As prophets are sent on Earth to help men work out their physical karma, so I have been directed by God to serve on an astral planet as a savior. It is called *Hiranyaloka* or 'Illuminated Astral Planet.' There I am aiding advanced beings to rid themselves of astral karma and thus attain liberation from astral rebirths. The dwellers of Hiranyaloka are highly developed spiritually; all of them had acquired, in their last earth-incarnation, the meditation-given power of consciously leaving their physical bodies at death."

TRAVELING IN THE BODY OF LIGHT

A GREAT MANY PEOPLE WRITE to me at my newspaper and Internet columns and claim to have traveled outside their bodies. Out-of-body experiences (OBEs) are surprisingly common. Surveys have yielded differing results showing that between twenty-five and sixty percent of people questioned claimed to have experienced an OBE. Whatever the true figure, it is clear from surveys, and my bulging mailbag, that this is certainly not an uncommon experience. Here is an example from one of the many thousands of letters and e-mails sent to me:

"A few years ago I had an extremely painful operation without anesthetic," a woman wrote. "I left the hospital twenty minutes after the surgery in a state of shock, anger, and mixed emotions. My center of vision suddenly changed. I stood about three stories higher, above myself, looking down at the scene below. I could see the pedestrians walking by, the cars and buses, the flat rooftops of the buildings. I even saw myself stop at the curb, look both ways, and cross the street."

She went on, "I have a bald spot on the top of my head, and I noticed that there was a small scar on it that I did not know was there!"

This is an unusual case because the OBE happened while she was walking along the street. Celia Green, a U.K. psychical investigator, cites a couple of cases in which motorcyclists left their bodies while driving at high speed. (Fortunately, they did not have accidents.) Pilots have also had similar experiences, finding themselves apparently outside their aircraft struggling to get in. One of the most famous examples of this happened to Charles A. Lindbergh in 1927 as he made the first ever flight across the Atlantic in his plane the *Spirit of St. Louis*: "I existed independently of time and matter. I felt myself departing from my body as I imagine a spirit would depart—emanating into the cockpit, extending through the fuselage as though no frame of fabric walls were there, angling upward, outward, until I reformed in an awareness far distant from the human form I left in a fast-flying transatlantic plane. But I remained connected to my body through a long-extended strand, a strand so tenuous that it could have been severed by a breath."

Most out-of-body experiences happen spontaneously. Often a period of severe stress or shock or fatigue can induce the astral body to temporarily separate from the physical body. Reports also come from people who say they have had an OBE while they were resting, sleeping, or dreaming. The majority of OBEs occur when people are in bed, ill, or resting, with a smaller percentage coming while the person is drugged or medicated. There is a high incidence of out-of-body experience during puberty. Of course, some of these "experiences" may be fantasy, but there are a great many cases on record now that give empirical proof that such experiences do exist, because the astral traveler has seen and described things from the journey that he or she could not have known. For example, out-of-body travelers have read off numbers from random-number generating machines placed in a room separate from their physical bodies, or seen target objects placed at a distance, even on the roofs of buildings.

21

WHAT TO DO IF YOU LEAVE YOUR BODY

"Life is pleasant. Death is peaceful. It's the transitions that's troublesome."

—ISAAC ASIMOV (SCIENCE FICTION WRITER, 1920–1992)

THE EXPERIENCE OF LEAVING THE physical body is usually a pleasurable one. I have had a number of OBEs myself, and it always feels natural and is an enjoyable experience. However, my first OBE, which happened to me during my adolescence, was frightening. As I was falling asleep, I felt myself rise to the ceiling. I looked around and saw myself on the bed. My immediate thought was that I had died in my sleep, and I panicked. Instantaneously, there was a feeling of great shaking, and I felt myself shoot back into my body like a whip being lashed. There was a huge bang and a flash of light, and I awoke with my body drenched in cold sweat.

Nowadays, if the same thing happens, I remain calm and enjoy the experience of being free of the body. I realize that it is a natural experience and is safe to consciously practice. There may be those, perhaps, who have had "one OBE too many" and ended up in the spirit world permanently. Being dead, they would have no conventional way to let us know what had happened! That said, however, through experience I believe OBEs to be safe, because I know of no cases where communicating spirits have warned against it. Also, there have been no reported cases of people dying while practicing OBE experiments under laboratory conditions.

It is possible to induce an out-of-body experience. These are described in detail in my other books: *The Hidden Meaning of*

Dreams and *Remembering Your Dreams*, also published by Sterling. The simplest methods of OBE induction require you to deliberately relax very deeply and visualize that you are being pulled toward a point in the room, such as a light fixture. As the physical mechanism of the body becomes quiescent, the body of light continues to remain active. Instead of resting in the physical body, it goes out of the body and into the astral plane. The body of light lays aside the physical body like we lay aside our clothes. It is also possible to use lucid dream techniques to trigger astral flight.

If you take a nap and find yourself out of your body, don't panic. Enjoy the experience. It is likely, at first, to last only moments, but with practice the experience can be sustained. Some mystical teachings say that everyone astral travels every night—it's just that we forget that we've done it once we wake up. Part of the art of astral travel is being able to recall the experience when you return to the body. If you have used a sleep technique, you may lose awareness of the experience in the same way you forget your dreams upon waking.

Traveling in the body of light is easy, provided one practices. It takes perseverance and patience.

Initially, you may indulge yourself in the enjoyable sensations that arise as you free yourself of your physical form. The physical body feels sluggish in comparison to its astral counterpart. It is like clay compared to light. The body of light is pure life force.

You may see your physical body laid on the bed as I did and decide now is the time to venture further afield. Perhaps you will travel to places you know, or move to far-off countries on the other side of the world. Imagine the feeling of soaring high above the world and seeing the landscape moving below you!

When I was a young man, my grandfather was very ill. Coming close to death, he spoke to me about an experience he had while in the hospital. His eyes were shining with delight and excitement as he spoke. "My whole bed lifted up and floated down the corridor over there," he said. "It was wonderful. I flew out of the hospital and all over the world. I even saw the continent of Australia laid out below me. Craig, I will never be afraid of dying. You must never fear death." Those few words, from someone so close to me and whom I could trust implicitly, had a profound effect upon me.

MEDITATION — PRACTICE FOR THE REAL THING

"Philosophy is a rehearsal for death."

—PLATO

THE MEDITATION PRACTICE GIVEN here will help you to familiarize yourself with what happens when you leave your body in preparation for entry to the spirit world. It can be done now, as you read through the instructions below, or read aloud for group practice. After you read each segment, pause awhile, so that you can experience the feelings and images from your unconscious. This gentle approach will enable you to become more attuned to the dying experiences that are already logged within your unconscious from earlier incarnations. Becoming aware of these things in a gentle and controlled way, you will be more prepared to leave the earth experience when your time comes. You will be more able to let go of your fear and move toward the light in a spirit of joyful expectation.

Meditation Exercise: Experiencing the Afterlife

This is going to be an enjoyable experience. Relax and breathe deeply. As you breathe in, feel yourself fill with life-giving energy. As you breathe out, feel yourself relax more deeply. Notice how good you feel as you relax. Let go of all worry and stress. Wrap yourself in the soothing warmth of relaxation. Feel the whole body relax from the tips of your toes to the top of your head. Enjoy this feeling for a minute or two.

Now imagine that your body is laid on a bed. Everything around you is peaceful and still as you observe your body. See it from every perspective: from above, from the feet, from the side, and from the head. You can hear the lungs breathing and may want to reach out and touch the body with your astral hands. Look at your bodily form and especially the face. The face has a neutral expression. How do you feel about what you see? Is it really you? Would you be prepared to leave it behind? Consider these things for a moment.

Now imagine that your body is dead. You are still able to look at it. You notice that the breathing has stopped. Knowing that you are the observer of the body, are you concerned that it has ceased functioning? Look at the body again. You touch it and notice that it is cold. There is a pallor to the face. Is it you? What feelings do you have as you clearly see it? Are you prepared to let go? Consider these things for a moment.

You now move away from the body and become aware of the entire room. You are a disembodied point of consciousness so you can view the room from wherever you like. How does it feel to have no body? You may experience a feeling of joy and release as you realize that you are free of the body's whims and demands. You may have the sensation of being as light as a soap bubble that floats in the breeze. You are an ex-physical! Observe your feelings and the sensations that come to you.

Now you hear below you the sound of voices. The people that you love are gathered around the body that you have discarded. You realize that you cannot only see and hear them but you can also "hear" their thoughts and "feel" their feelings. You have complete telepathy, but it is only a one-way communication. No matter what you do, your family and friends below remain oblivious to your presence. Their thoughts rise like great white clouds. What do you "hear" from your loved ones? Does their grief make you feel uncomfortable? Perhaps you want to tell them that you are okay. They should not be so concerned because you have only discarded the body. Think also about the time you lost somebody you loved. Did you send them positive thoughts to speed them on their journey, or were the thoughts you sent full of despair and grief?

Clearly this is the most difficult emotional part of the dying experience. We are irrevocably bound by feelings of love to people in this world. To let go of this attachment will inevitably be accompanied by a feeling of severing from what we hold dear.

At this point, our higher self will make us aware that nothing is really lost. We will all certainly be reunited, and time isn't a concern. The experience of time in the spirit world is different from earthly time. Although earthly time is linear, spirit time is happening all at once. You'll have a sense of its passage, but for you time will move quickly, or slowly, depending upon your need. A long separation from the ones you love can seem no more than a blink of the eye. Imagine now that an angel is with you. This could be your spirit guide or a symbol of your higher self in the guise of a winged being, if you prefer. The angel whispers in your ear. What words of comfort does the angel say to you?

Have you ever felt stirred while listening to great music, or been overwhelmed by the magnificent beauty of a landscape? This feeling of inspiration will now fill you as you release yourself from the earthly plane. Simultaneously, you will have a feeling of ineffable love as you move toward the heavenly plane. Remember the most important feeling of love you had in life, and multiply it by a million times. This is the love you will feel. This is divine love. It fills you with an irresistible urge to move toward it. It appears like a light.

You now move toward the light. As you leave the material realm, what feelings do you have? Have you accomplished what you set out to do? Have you made others happy and created empathy and love? Is the world you leave behind a better place for your having been there? Are there things that you would like to have done, or perhaps would like to have done better?

Now let go of all of these feelings and doubts, and let them merge with the light. Allow yourself to become at one with this wonderful state that is all around you. Everywhere you look there is light. Light upon light upon light. All is divine love, divine light. Let go, into the light.

The above meditation may have stimulated many emotions and made you think about your life and its objectives. It should help you to see the impermanence of the body and all material things. However, the feelings you received highlight what is most important to you in this life. You may have had the feeling that there is still much remaining undone. Perhaps you felt that the most important things are not the day-to-day cares and material goals, but matters of the heart. Are there ways that you can improve your earthly life so that, when you look back next time, you will feel that you have come closer to completing your earthly life satisfactorily?

MOVING BEYOND THE EARTH PLANE

"When man is about to leave the world, as leave he must, he is surrounded by his family who lament, 'What is to happen to us when you leave?' but the poor fellow is confronted by a more personal problem, 'What is to happen to me?' In fact, if he tried he could have known the reality and gone with a smile. Men are born with a helpless lamenting cry; they should die with a smile of happy joy. That is the purpose of the years between."

—Sathya Sai Baba

Western theology has, I believe, made a mistake when it talks about the afterlife as being a place or places. It is natural for us to think in terms of objective existence, even when a life separate from the material world is being considered. Many people think of heaven as a place situated somewhere in space. This idea has existed since earliest times, when people thought the spirit became a star in the night sky or descended into the bowels of the earth. They saw the heavenly worlds as a place filled with beautiful buildings encrusted with jewels and situated in a landscape of endless flowing gardens.

However, heaven is not a place, it is a "state." Most mediums describe these states as planes of existence.

This world, here and now, is also a plane of existence. For example, you are seated reading this book. You can feel its pages and see its shape and are able to read these words. Yet, in reality, what you are perceiving is a picture inside your head. You are receiving information from your five senses that is being processed at lightning speed by the brain to construct a view of reality. The image before your eyes is actually created from signals from the back of the retina. And it is actually created by the eye's lens upside down. The brain turns the picture back around the right way for us. Similarly, you may have been unaware of the sounds around you—until I mention it to you now. The ticking of a mechanical clock, the muffled sound of the neighbor's TV set, a siren in the distance, all sounds are wiped from your consciousness while you concentrate. Often we are not aware of the repeated sound of a clock . . . until it stops!

My point is that we only perceive a small part of the world at any time. For example, I used to be an artist and trained myself to have a better awareness of color. If I glance at, say, a flowering plant, I may be immediately aware of the beauty of the blossoms themselves. However, if I open my awareness, I may also notice the form each blossom takes and the subtleties of color, how the leaves and stems relate to the flowers and to each other, and the spacing left between. I may also notice the unity of pattern made by the structure of the stems or see the intricate patterns in the texture of the petals or leaves. If I open my awareness still further, I may see the auric field of the plant and sense the life force that radiates from it. If I allow my perceptions to fully unfold, I may momentarily become aware of the transcendent beauty of a particular flower and its divine form.

Is the world that I am seeing now the same as the world that everyone else sees? The truth is that we all exist in different states of consciousness and shift between higher and lower levels of perception. Medication, meditation, excitement, nodding off, inebriation, fright, and boredom—all affect our consciousness and perceptions. How would someone in these states view the bowl of flowers? If I were feeling gloomy or depressed, I would probably be less aware of the beauty of the flowers, for my attention would be focused on my own feelings and thoughts. If I am in love, the colors

29

of the flowers may appear to be more alive, and the whole world may look bright. The truth is, we all live in completely different worlds and move between different worlds all the time. Is there any reason why our perceptions can't be widened to include the afterworld through working to improve psychic awareness?

Jesus of Nazareth spoke of the next life with the authority of someone who had traveled there. He said, "In my Father's house are many mansions: if it were not so, I would have told you." I believe, in those words, he is giving us a glimpse of an unlimited range of planes of existence and levels of consciousness attainable in the higher realms of being. In the afterlife, the nature of objective reality is different from what we know here. It changes according to our level of consciousness.

I will explain this in detail in a moment, but first it is important to understand a little more about awareness and the independent existence of the spirit.

THOUGHTS HAVE WINGS

"Has anyone supposed it lucky to be born?
I hasten to inform him or her it is as lucky to die, and I know it.
I pass death with the dying, and birth with the new-washed babe
. . . .
and am not contained between my hat and boots."
—WALT WHITMAN

MATERIALISTS ASSUME THAT THE brain is not only the generator of consciousness but that thoughts are limited to the electrical impulses that jump between the synapses. All thoughts—and awareness itself—are contained within the space between the ears. When we die, that's it! The lights are switched off, and there's no one at home.

So, when psychics claim that extrasensory perception (ESP) is a fact and that we can, for example, share thoughts across a distance, it is met with a strong negative response by most scientists. The ferocity of their counterclaims is understandable, for if what we say is true, then it will turn the whole of the materialistic view of the universe on its head. The authority of science would tumble like a statue of Lenin in Moscow.

It is a brave scientist who takes ESP seriously.

My television work has often seen me cross swords with skeptics, and I have taken great pleasure doing experiments on the air. One person who, I feel it is fair to say, was floored by what I can do is the skeptical psychologist Dr. Richard Wiseman. As skeptics go, he is an amicable person, but he believes that people like myself are either complete fakes or that what we do can be explained by simple psychological rules.

In my earlier book *The Psychic Casebook* (Sterling), I quote a case in which Dr. Wiseman and I are pitched against one another. For the *Magic and Mystery Show* a séance is set up in a darkened room. Dr. Wiseman brings in a guest whom I know nothing about—the British television host Nick Knowles, who was, at that time, completely unknown to me. There was no way I could have learned who the guest would be in advance, and so have the opportunity to research his background. Dr. Wiseman saw to it that there was no cheating.

I gave a spirit message to Nick Knowles. As I linked in, I could tell that Nick didn't know many people who had died, but I felt someone draw close to me who was really important to him. "There's a young man you know in the spirit," I said. "He liked motorcycles."

"Yes," replied Nick, as Dr. Wiseman sat next to me scribbling notes.

"He tells me that he died in Australia and that his name is ____ ____."

Nick nearly fell off his seat as I gave him the full name of his friend, whose grave he had specially visited in Australia.

"He says that he was recently engaged to a girl called ____ before he died. Her birthday is ____. He sends his love and talks about children by the names of ____ and ____."

Everything I said was right on. Richard Wiseman struggled to counter my reading. I gave only the correct names, so he couldn't argue that I had thrown in so many names that one or two were bound to be right. Fortunately, the facts given to me by the spirit were straightforward and could be quickly validated by Nick Knowles. This was clear evidence of mediumship that was exceptionally hard to dismiss.

I crossed swords once again with Dr. Wiseman, for a show hosted by Granada Television in the United Kingdom. I was to demonstrate telepathy. The audience was to watch a film clip, and I was to describe what they were watching.

The film clip was chosen by the producers and kept secret from everyone. This silent clip was then shown to the audience, who attempted to "send" the picture to me by telepathy while I sat blindfolded.

Without hesitation, I was able to say that I saw motorbikes crashing in a race. Again, straight to the point. For my next demonstration on the show, I stood in front of the audience and told individuals there things about themselves. I told them about their jobs and where they came from, and even gave two of the people the numbers that they regularly played for the national lottery.

I am fortunate in being able to access my telepathic ability. However, in the spirit world everyone has unlimited telepathic ability. You can share thoughts and feelings with complete clarity. You understand that this means, of course, that never again will you be able to say, "My wife doesn't understand me."

Much of the information that mediums are given about the afterlife is transmitted by the people of the spirit through the use of telepathy.

GETTING YOUR MESSAGE ACROSS

When you first arrive in the spirit world, it will take you a little while to get used to using telepathy. At first, it will appear as if people are talking to you normally, since this is the method of communication that you are used to. However, you will then notice that it only "appears" that they are talking. You are "hearing" their thoughts as spoken words. Similarly, you will notice that your own thoughts and feelings are completely transparent. The first spirit people you meet will "hear" your words as your thoughts form, before the words actually leave your mouth.

The same form of telepathic communication is used to communicate with the material plane. Unfortunately, you will find that most of the people you may try to communicate with are completely oblivious to your communications. Some may interpret your thoughts and sense, see, or even smell you. However, if you want to get a detailed message across, you will need to find someone who is telepathic and, most important, is aware of the telepathic signals from you and your spirit friends.

A medium is used by the spirit people as a vehicle for communication between the two worlds. Onlookers assume that the medium is able to see the spirit person standing near them and can hear their voice speaking to them. Some mediums encourage this belief by saying things such as "I can see so-and-so standing by you" or "He is saying such-and-such." This is not actually true.

Mental mediums perceive the spirit communicator inwardly. When we say we hear a voice, it is an inner voice that we hear. You may hear a tune inside your head or remember the voice of someone speaking—this is very similar to the way mediums hear the spirit. The name given for this type of spirit communication is *clairaudience*. Intuitive clairaudience is a subtle condition that can be described as listening-in to soundless words. The medium is aware of an impression of hearing, as word forms come into consciousness.

Similarly, a medium feels sensations when a spirit is communicating. For example, I may feel the physical conditions the spirit had when on earth. I will sense which sex the spirit was or get impressions of the personality. This sensing is called *clairsentience*. Finally, I may see mental effigies showing the events from the spirit person's life, see his or her face, or perhaps see pictures of places that were important to the person. This perception of images is usually called *clairvoyance*. (Strictly speaking, clairvoyance is defined by parapsychology as an aspect of extrasensory perception in which an object or event is perceived without the use of the known senses.)

Mental mediumship, therefore, comes from a combination of inner sensing, seeing, and hearing. Put all of these impressions together and it is possible to give an accurate description of the person who has passed over to spirit. Occasionally, when the power is high, the inner impressions are so strong that I may hear, see, or feel a presence as clearly as if the spirit stood near me, like a solid person from this world. However, I recognize that even these powerful impressions are, in fact, coming from within me. Objective mediumship, where you may see a spirit standing in a room is, in fact, intuitive mediumship. For example, if a person professes to see a ghost, it may actually be an impression made upon the mind that gives the spirit the "appearance" of being part of the environment. What you see is, in fact, a thought picture being impressed by a spirit onto your or the medium's consciousness. (Objective mediumship is not to be confused with physical mediumship, where the spirit manifests through ectoplasm produced by the medium.)

So, where do these mental impressions come from? It has been argued that mediums are simply reading the memories of their sitters through telepathy. As quoted above, people like me are able to demonstrate telepathy and can even describe a piece of film being watched by an audience. So is it not possible that all mediumship is just telepathy? Could it be that mediumship has nothing to do with the afterlife but is merely the perception of memories using this sixth sense, telepathy?

It is true that a good deal of telepathy happens when mediums give a consultation. I may begin by telling my sitter about what he or she has been doing that day or about things that are on the sitter's mind. This helps me to link with the sitter's vibration and enables a flow of energy between our auras. Once a flow of energy is established between us, it is then possible for the spirit communicator to influence my thoughts. Telepathy does take place, not between the sitter and me but between the spirit communicator and me.

Of course, not everything you see at a sitting, demonstration, or Spiritualist meeting is true mediumship. For example, I recently went to a Spiritualist church with my wife, Jane, and daughter, Danielle, to see one of "England's finest Spiritual artists." A female medium stood on the rostrum and gave a demonstration of shallow mediumship while a male medium sat scribbling a portrait. We all waited eagerly to see the portrait that he worked on with great concentration while she made a spirit communication.

Finally, the tension was over and the long-awaited picture was revealed to the audience. The psychic artist had drawn a man who looked just like Freddie Kruger from the movie *Nightmare on Elm Street*! (Or so it seemed to my family and me.) But perhaps the most amazing thing was that someone in the audience accepted it as a picture of someone he knew! The next picture was even more unusual. Danielle (age eleven) decided it looked like the Marshmallow Man in the film *Ghostbusters* and had trouble keeping a straight face.

That experience combined bad mediumship and bad drawing. However, even good mediumship is questionable if it can be proven to be only mind reading. I often find that it's the things that are not accepted at a consultation that usually prove to be the most significant evidence.

Sometimes the recipient of the spirit message has to check the facts with a third party who was not present at the consultation. If the information is then proven to be correct, it demonstrates that the medium was not reading the sitter's mind.

Sally Colverson felt a little embarrassed when everything I said was wrong. "Craig gave me a message from a man called Mr. Williams who had persistent breathing conditions and a bad limp. 'I feel that there is a link with South Wales in the U.K.,' said Craig, 'and you will understand the name George associated with this name. It's not the man's Christian name; rather, it's the name of his friend who lived next door. The street is full of terraced houses. It's either called Church Street or Chapel Street—both names feel significant. I can hear a brass band playing. It was so loud the dogs would howl. Lots of dogs howling. I can hear lots of dogs.'

"Craig had drawn a blank. Everything except the link with

Wales was wrong. He looked a little embarrassed as he moved to his next link. However, when I got home I asked my dad about the names I had been given. 'This is way before your time,' said Dad. 'George and Mr. Williams were my neighbors when I lived in Old Church Place. Mr. Williams was a Spiritualist. He suffered from chest problems and had a limp due to infantile paralysis. It was me that was in the band, and we used to always annoy the neighbors—only George and Mr. Williams supported us. We played at the Miner's Hall. Problem was, it would always set the dogs howling at the nearby breeders in Chapel Street.' "

Cases like this demonstrate that mediumship is not telepathy.

HOW TO COMMUNICATE THROUGH MEDIUMS

When you are dead you may get the opportunity to communicate through a medium. A little learning now about the art of spirit communication may help you a great deal when you enter the next life.

Mediums cannot make a spirit person communicate. We have to open our awareness and see what comes. I am not like an open telephone line to the other side. What happens is a form of telepathy, not between me and the person with me but between the person in the spirit world and me. I "see," "hear," and "feel" the spirit—you will remember that we call these faculties clairvoyance, clairaudience, and clairsentience. By putting these impressions together, I am able to build a picture of the communicator and prove that the human personality survives death.

If you were a spirit person now, what would you say to someone you loved to prove that you were actually you? Imagine you find yourself on the spirit side of life and are able to use your mind telepathically. Suddenly you realize that you are aware of ("hear") the thoughts of a medium asking his or her spirit guides for assistance in communicating. You may even sense the medium's anxiety about getting the facts right. Surrounding you, the medium's spirit guides and helpers are ready to help you project your thoughts—to use your mind to influence the medium's mind.

When you send a thought to the medium, you quickly learn that he or she is not a clear channel. Although you can communicate with full clarity telepathically with other people in the spirit world, it is a difficult process communicating with the living. You may say (or rather think) "My name's Jack," but as soon as the thought is received, the medium's own mind alters it.

"Mac?" the medium's mind offers as message. "Is this part of the name? Or someone who used an Apple Mac computer? Or loved Big Mac hamburgers?" You immediately realize it is not going to be as easy as you thought. In a way, it's like the party game of a spoken message passed down a long line of people. By the time the last person gets the message, the meaning has almost surely changed beyond recognition. This is a particular problem for mediums who are just beginning or for psychics who have had little or no mediumistic training. As mediumship skills advance, it becomes much clearer whether words and impressions received are actually spirit directed or figments of the self.

Fortunately, communication between the worlds is not always as bad as the example given. Sometimes, if a medium is completely open and keeps a still mind, it is possible to convey thoughts with clarity. However, you will soon discover—the medium's spirit guides will help you—that it is easier to plant ideas into the medium's mind using feelings and images than words and numbers. You need to project your "personality" into the medium's mind so he or she can relate to the sitter the type of person you are. Once this is accepted, you can also give him easy-to-see images or pictures of places and scenes from your life. What pictures and impressions would you provide to prove that you are, indeed, you and not someone else?

The spirit guides will be aware of the medium's interests and knowledge. For example, the medium may love music and have a wide musical knowledge. If this is the case, you may be able to project to him your favorite tune, or one of the tunes played at your funeral. A medium with a good knowledge of music is more likely to "get" the tune you are giving him. Similarly, if the medium has a good sense of direction and a knowledge of geography, you may be able to more easily show him places that were important to you in life. A memory of the streets of Paris, France, for example, may be recognized by the medium, who is then able to name this city as being significant to you.

The famous spirit healer Harry Edwards likened mediumistic communication to a violin: "If the instrument is a poor one, it is reflected in the musical tones that come from it. The result also reflects the musician's intimacy and knowledge of how to use the violin. Give the master violinist a superb instrument, and the result is far different. Every good instrumentalist has to know his instrument, the feel of it, and this can only come through usage and experience. It is just the same with mediumship."

Given the inherent difficulties associated with spirit communication, what could you provide in order to, as much as possible, specifically identify you as the spirit communicator? Supposedly, you can't give your usual basic information (name, address, identification number) because the medium's mind is not receptive to this type of information. With the communication limited to sensations and visual impressions, what could you give to the medium?

You would have to work within the limitations the mediumship naturally imposes. For example, the medium may be able to sense whether you were a man or a woman when on earth. You could also easily project feelings of your stature and your physical mannerisms. The medium may even mimic these unconsciously as the sitting progresses. Similarly, you could give the impressions that you felt before you died. You may be able to project sensations that describe the progress of your illness and your passing. If there was an accident, you may be able to give the impression of traveling at great speed prior to a crash, falling from a height, or being hit by something. This type of impression is more easily perceived by the medium and translated into meaningful messages to the sitter. Of course, since your bodily death, you are free of pain and disease, but the reality of it is likely to be something that is still very much on the mind of the sitter. Most important, evidence you are able to provide as to how you passed over can stand as proof that it is you communicating. You may also be able to give the sitter reassurance that you are now free of suffering.

While you are communicating, it is up to the medium to keep his mind as clear as possible and not interfere with or try to make sense of the impressions being sent to him. I have noticed, in my own mediumship, that things go awry as soon as I attempt to "take hold," interfering with the impressions I am getting. When I, in the midst of receiving mode, try to make logical sense of the pictures and sensations, I mess up. Quality mediumship is an uninterrupted, uncensored flow of information. As I jokingly, and rather grossly, tell my pupils: "Accurate mediumship is like verbal diarrhea! Just let it flow."

PROVING THE SURVIVAL OF YOUR PERSONALITY

Your personality doesn't go though a massive transformation when you go to the spirit. Actually, you remain comparatively unchanged.

Some of your cherished beliefs may be undermined, but the fundamental qualities of your personality remain fixed. Sadly, you will not become a demigod, even though your loved ones on earth may begin to idealize you as such—no matter what they thought of you when you were with them—since now you have seemingly all-knowing messages to pass to them from the beyond.

No, grumpy old Uncle Bill will still be grumpy old Uncle Bill when he gets to the spirit world. If he was a grumbling old fart in this life, he will remain so in the world beyond. The human personality doesn't change very quickly during our earthly life, and there are no sudden transformations either when we enter the spirit state. We may become more aware of our faults and have a clearer insight into ourselves and the mistakes we made during life, but the human personality itself remains relatively unchanged.

If you think about your own nature, how much have you changed since you were a teenager? You may be a little mellower in your behavior, but the fundamental qualities that make up your personality probably haven't changed a great deal. It takes "spiritual" effort to bring about a metamorphosis of the personality. Changing ourselves into more spiritually aware beings is, in my opinion, the reason we have been given access to earthly bodies. This is the objective of most spiritual disciplines, and for most people, the changes within only one lifetime are marginal.

You can therefore imagine how much more difficult communication gets if grumpy old Uncle Bill is the spirit communicator. Not only must the message get through the interference of the medium's mind and the blocks created by the sitter's own aura, but we also have to get Uncle Bill's participation. He may be very stubborn and not like being asked to speak. Similarly, he may not have said much in life and is not especially inclined to be more talkative from the spirit plane. Too, many spirit communicators can become quite shy about speaking out!

If you ever try communicating through a medium when you are dead, you will soon realize that it is a tricky business. In addition to the personalities involved, you have to slow your astral vibration in order to "sink" to the earth plane. You next have to attune your consciousness with the mind of the medium. This spiritual overshadowing is a difficult astral art that may require practice and instruction from the spirit helpers of the medium. It is also a strange experience to the newly dead to feel the inner world blend with the inner world of the medium, who becomes aware of your whole personality and earth memories. (Think mind-meld.) It's a job to keep any skeletons in the closet when communicating telepathically!

THE UNBORN SELF

In order for telepathic communication to take place between someone in the spirit world and the medium living on earth, it is necessary that a common state exists for them to work through. Some Spiritualists and mystics have called this the "mirror mind."

Nobody knows for certain how consciousness is created or sustained. From the brain's part, consciousness does not appear to be limited to any one place in it. It appears to be generated by the whole brain working together. Some scientists believe that the idea of consciousness and free will are, in fact, an illusion. For example, it has been discovered by measuring brain activity that the intention to do something comes "after" the brain has already decided to do it. The unconscious parts of the brain make decisions before "you" do. Our behavior is therefore guided not by free will but by subconscious processing. Professor Susan Greenfield claims: "The feeling of 'you'—the individual in your head—could well be the most impressive trick the brain plays. Somehow, the brain creates the illusion of a conscious self in control of its actions, while the true controlling force is the subconscious."

The medium's view is quite different. The brain is an organ of perception for creating images from the sensations that come from the five senses. It makes sense of the material world by generating images of reality. In many ways, the brain is similar to the computer I am using to write this book. If the computer goes wrong, or gets a virus, then my words may be destroyed or jumbled. If things go really bad, the machine may crash or become completely unusable. However, *I* am not the computer. The computer is my means of processing and communicating information and ideas. Add a modem and camera and it becomes a means of perception as well. The brain is an immense organic computer, but *I* am not the brain.

I have already spoken about telepathy, the ability of people to share thoughts through something other than the normal five senses. In your everyday life, you may "know" when someone is about to telephone you, or you may sense a person's mood before you see his or her face. If you are proficient at telepathy, you may be able to perceive much more detailed information. This would indicate that thought is not limited to the confines of the brain but can extend beyond it. Telepathy is a fact, and there is a great deal of proof to show that the whole of human consciousness can exist beyond the body.

Extrasensory perception and out-of-body experiences illustrate that it is possible for consciousness to exist independently of the body. My own view is that the brain is just our doorway into the material world. Human consciousness is not limited to the brain but extends in all directions. The extent of the reach of consciousness may be limitless.

Mediums believe that we are not prisoners of the brain. We are free. When we die, we live independently of the brain as, even now, part of us lives independently of the body. A portion of our consciousness is unborn and exists permanently in the spirit world. It may be the source of our sense of identity. I believe that I am able to do mediumship because I am in touch with this part of my being. I can blend with it simply by looking within myself.

The spirit people talk to me via this unborn self.

SPOOKS, GHOSTS, AND THE EARTH PLANE

"He who's not busy being born is busy dying."

—BOB DYLAN

SOON WE WILL CONSIDER THE afterlife itself and its many planes of existence. However, first I want to explain what happens to the earthly astral shell of the dying person, and about those souls who cling to the earth plane and do not immediately travel down that tunnel of light into the afterlife planes. I hope, also, to clear up one or two misconceptions about ghosts and phantoms, and perhaps reassure you that you are unlikely to spend eternity haunting the room in which you died or rattling chains in some spooky mansion.

WHAT TO DO IF YOU GET STUCK BETWEEN WORLDS

You take the corner a little too fast and break a little harder than you should. Now the steering has a mind of its own. You try to compensate, but it's too late. You've hit the curb, and now you are hurtling down a steep embankment. At this speed you may be dead in an instant.

When it happened to me, it felt as if someone had pulled the plug on reality. The world slowed down to an almost dead stop. "So this is it," I thought; yet I was surprisingly calm within. It was the classic my-life-flashed-before-me scenario. All the important events and people in my life filled my head simultaneously. In the same moment, I understood all the things I wanted to achieve in the world and within myself. Just before the car hit the bottom, an unruffled thought took sovereignty: "I wonder what comes next?"

Fortunately, the actual crash was cushioned by undergrowth, and I had no severe, much less fatal, injuries. Only my hands were badly bruised. I'd gripped the steering wheel so hard that I had bent it to the dashboard. My passenger, however, completely freaked out.

It's understandable. The shock of the sudden and unexpected event took him over the edge, so to speak. In those few seconds while I had contemplated my life, he explained later, he had left his body and run frantically through the woods ahead of the car. In the area of the crash, he felt himself running and running forever through the dark forest.

Now, suppose that the accident had been far worse and we had been killed. Or suppose it had happened to you. What would be the immediate experience of the afterlife plane?

During the moments before death, most people have a sense of calmness and acceptance. They are then drawn into a tunnel of light and through it into another world. However, for some, the shock of their death is so great they do not even realize they have reached that state. Would you panic at the end? Perhaps your spirit, on the order of my unfortunate passenger, would continue for a time to run pell-mell through the woods at night—sparking fear in unwary travelers hiking through the woods.

In the unlikely event you "get stuck" on the earth plane, what would happen? At first, the world would appear the same as usual to you, until you notice . . . nobody is reacting to your presence. You speak, but no one seems to hear a word you say. You yell, repeatedly, but people simply carry on without noticing you. You shout, you hit at them, you try everything you can to get their attention—but nothing works. Even the people you really care about cannot see you. *Nobody* is watching you: it's paranoia in reverse!

Some spirits stay around like this for a short period of time. Often they are in a stupefied somnambulistic state, almost unaware of what has happened to them. Occasionally they are angry at their situation or try to rectify the things that went wrong. They may be concerned about unfinished business, such as the division of the legacy of their estate, or are determined to confront someone who may have been the cause of their death.

The shock of sudden death can create this earth-bound situation, but it is usually a very temporary state. Most new spirits soon realize what has happened and become aware of their guardian spirits and deceased loved ones. Once the newly departed spirit recognizes the situation for what it is, it is a simple matter for the guiding spirits to draw him or her fully into the light of the afterlife.

According to Taoist and Buddhist teachings, it is "craving" that holds a person to the earth plane. This could perhaps manifest as the desire to seek revenge or to, perhaps, hold on to material possessions. In China, Japan, and other Eastern countries, they call these spirits *hungry ghosts* because they continually seek satisfaction from things that can never satisfy them. The craving can take many forms. The spirit may crave revenge, crave to hold on to worldly fame and fortune, or simply crave to continue living in our world. For example, a spirit may have a powerful sexual urge but, being bodyless, he or she is unable to satisfy such compulsions. The spirit is willing, so to speak, but the body is gone. It is like having a hunger that can never be satisfied. Such hungry ghosts haunt the area under and on the earth, perpetually tormented by insatiable greed.

Many Eastern peoples believe that hungry ghosts can be nourished by offerings made during religious ceremonies. For example in Singapore, during the seventh month of the lunar year, there is a celebration similar to our Halloween, and it makes trick-or-treat look lame in comparison.

During this time, ghosts return to visit their living relatives. In most cases, this is a pleasant reunion, but there are also troublemakers. These are the souls of spirits who left behind no descendants, or who had less than harmonious relations with an ex-wife, ex-husband, even the occasional creditor. You would not want one of these ghosts as your friend.

Appeasing the hungry ghosts is said to ward off bad luck and attract good fortune. During the ceremonies, flaming dragon-shaped incense sticks are lit on the streets, and loud, exuberant music is played nightly in outdoor tents to entertain the spooky ancestors.

Offerings are made to the spirits by burning fake money called "Hell Money." However, if you need really good luck, it is advisable to burn something a little more adventurous, such as a new television set, a cellular phone, or pieces of expensive furniture—anything that might come in handy to the spirit in the afterlife and earn you a favor. A favorite offering is lucky "black gold," fetching prices as high as $13,000 a nugget. I'm sure that, if you were to watch this hullabaloo from the spirit world, you would smile at the holy-smoke barbecue being performed especially for you.

However, like our own Halloween, the rituals are just superstition and nonsense that hark back to the time when sacrifices were made to the gods and spirits. The occasion, however, gives the bereaved an opportunity to express socially their feelings for departed loved ones and enables them to do something about their grief. Similarly, it provides a focal point to enable the minds of those on earth and in the spirit to link for a time, and serves as an Eastern way of expressing remembrance, much as a Westerner puts flowers on a grave.

Throughout my many years working as a medium, I have very rarely encountered spirits that are said to be trapped. Yet, hundreds of people have claimed that they are being troubled by all sorts of fiendish phenomena. Most of the cases of haunting and possession that I have investigated turn out to be attention-seeking fantasies or, in some sad cases, the diseased imaginings of a latent schizophrenia.

I remember one gentleman who rang me with a very convincing story of how his house was haunted by strange elemental spirits. When I visited his home, he showed no signs of mental disturbance and behaved like any normal person. I asked him to take me to the area of the house where he felt the bad spirits were at their strongest. When he did, I felt nothing untoward in the room.

"I really do not think you have anything to worry about here," I said, hoping to put his mind at rest.

"But can't you feel them now?" he replied in an anxious tone. "They come from under the bed; please take a look!"

I lay on the floor and looked beneath the bed. "Can't you see them? There are armies of marching insects. Look, some are wearing uniforms!"

Lying there on the cold floor looking for uniformed insects under the bed in a strange man's house suddenly didn't seem like such a good idea. I made my apologies and left . . . just a tad more hastily than I normally would.

My numerous communications with the spirit world have revealed to me that even spirits who have been killed, murdered, or otherwise died suddenly have arrived at the other side without any hitches. However, extreme emotional states of mind at the moment of death can cause problems. For example, I worked with the U.K. police on one occasion and was asked if I could communicate with the spirit of a man who had been murdered above his shop.

I felt his spirit come close, and it explained how he had been stabbed in the stomach in the front room, but the killers had dragged his body through the hall and dumped his body facedown in the bath. I was also able to describe the woman who sat in the black getaway car, and I told the police that another red vehicle was parked at the back of the building. At that time, these facts, and many other details related to me by the spirit, had not been revealed to the press. I've never seen a police officer shake so much—particularly when I told him that he had once put the spirit communicator in jail.

The murdered man told us that for a while he had been trapped between the two worlds. He had panicked at the time of the murder. Much of the time he was trapped had been spent trying to tell his mother what had happened. He had even succeeded in moving objects in his mother's house trying to get her attention. He was absolutely furious about being murdered!

49

Against what he felt was his better nature, he ratted on the murderers via my mediumship and claimed that now he could move on into the next world. Much later, when the full story was revealed in the U.K. newspapers, the mother of the victim claimed that she had felt that the spirit of her son had been trying desperately to get in touch with her. She had seen objects in her home mysteriously move by themselves.

WHAT TRAMP SOULS DO WHEN THEY ARE DEAD

Feelings of anger and revenge can temporarily bind a spirit person to the earth plane. (Shock can also cause this, but only for a very short time.) The best thing to do, if you discover yourself wandering the earth plane as a spirit, is to recognize that it is your own desire that is holding you. You must "cut the ties that bind" you to this material plane. Let go of anger, resentment, fear, and revenge, and your spirit will quickly move toward the higher realms, where it belongs.

The process of letting go of this life is very hard for some people. Some spirits have such strong sensual attachments to the world that their only thought is to reenter physical form and continue their sensual enjoyments. In this case, they may try to possess the body and mind of a weak, mentally unstable individual. Such wandering spirits are what mediums call *tramp souls.*

Ordinarily, tramp souls are confined to their own sphere, in the same way we are limited to our material world. They exist on gloomy lower worlds and spend their days trying to rejoin the earth plane. Our world, which we see as full of color and light, looks hollow and dull to tramp souls; nonetheless, they cling to our world of shades.

Some tramp souls are filled with worry about the duties and tasks that remain unfulfilled from their time spent on earth. A few rare cases also attach themselves to those loved ones left behind, brooding over them and impotently striving to communicate with them.

Tramp souls who have done a great deal of wrong while on earth may spend time wandering the earth plane haunting scenes of their earthly transgressions. They may feel remorse and may try to make vain endeavors to undo or atone for their misdeeds. Usually these souls are not fully conscious of their predicament, acting somewhat like a somnambulist—not fully aware of our world or the next.

It is nonetheless very hard for earthbound astral beings to penetrate the earth plane and to harm us. Imagine what it would be like if they could. Most people would be living in abject terror all of the time. God has given us enough problems on this plane without adding the interference of evil spirits.

What tramp souls do when they are dead is wander around the earth plane and the lower planes in a state of perplexed semiconsciousness. They are unaware of the passage of time. Sometimes they may try to return to the world by revisiting the place where they died. When you pass into the spirit world it is likely that you will bypass this realm entirely and be completely unaware of it.

But don't lose sleep worrying about tramp souls, or whether someone has died in the room where you are reading this book. Your good vibrations protect you. They shine out from you like a cleansing light to safeguard you and your environment. The forces of darkness cannot penetrate the light. In particular, God is the highest spirit of all and acts as invincible protection. Tramp souls cannot stand the high vibrations of spiritual thought. If you ever have worries about evil spirits, just set your thoughts, without fear, on God.

Similarly, if we wish to help these souls, we can project thoughts of light and love. Thoughts become positive energies that help souls to rise to their proper plane of astral existence. When mediums or "rescue circles" help these souls, we send strong, reassuring thoughts to encourage the lost spirit to progress into the higher sphere. Even when their soul grieves and weeps, we still insist the soul awaken and do its duty by going on to the spirit abode. Eventually, the soul making this resolve lets go of its grip upon this world. It will see a loving spirit, such as its mother or a guardian angel, come to release it from its self-imposed bondage. Once it sees the light of the spirit, the soul will soar to the heavenly realms.

Collective negative thought has the opposite effect. It can attract spirits from the lower planes and allow all sorts of mischief to occur. It may also attract spirits from the lower realm of the astral, "below" even the realm of the tramp souls.

AN OPEN DOOR TO MISCHIEVOUS SPIRITS

In the hands of a well-trained medium or Spiritualist, the Ouija board can be a useful tool, and there are many interesting cases on record where the board has given useful and empirical information. For example, it was in the use of a Ouija board that, at a séance in St. Louis in 1913, a spirit announced itself as an entity named Patience Worth. By this method, the entity also dictated several interesting historical novels whose insight into past eras still intrigue historians, who felt those insights were beyond the capacities of the medium through whom the novels were received.

I personally find the Ouija board a tedious and inaccurate way to communicate with the spirit world. There seems to be very little point once you have developed mediumship. However, it is a method that appeals to those who want to take a shortcut to spirit communication. Using it, it is possible to communicate with the people you love who have passed on. Because the method is so tied to the energies of the earth plane, however, it also throws open the door to every spirit that wants to "log on." Without a powerful medium in control, using the Ouija board is a spiritual minefield. I'm reminded of one consultation in which it was revealed by the sitter that her son and some teenagers had been playing with the Ouija board. What started out as a way of relieving boredom took on a sinister turn when the board spelled out that all five of the boys present would die. In just over a week, one boy was dead, and two others had since died in tragic circumstances.

The mother of the first boy, age seventeen, told me, "When my son told his dad and me he was going to die, we thought he was joking. We had no idea he and his four friends had been messing with the Ouija board." Soon after, on New Year's Eve, her son was attacked and, during the fight, his head was banged against the pavement several times.

"My son collapsed a few days after the fight, while babysitting for my other son's children. He was rushed to the hospital and put on life support. On the tenth day, pneumonia set in, and he just slipped away.

"A few months later, one of the other boys caught pneumonia while camping and died. It was a shock, as he'd been so healthy. That's when one of my son's friends came to see us. He was in total panic and told us about the Ouija board. It all seemed so ridiculous to us. But this year, another of the group took his own life, leaving only two out of the five."

During the consultation with the mother, who also saw my wife, Jane, we were able to advise her that the other boys would be okay. This was the work of mischievous spirits, and it need not become a self-fulfilling prophecy. The others would be fine. Some years have passed since this case, and the other two boys continue to thrive.

A properly developed and trained medium will keep his or her mind and soul centered on the higher truths and resist the temptation to meddle with the phenomena of the lower states. Mediumship, practiced with love and light, can be of great benefit to the world and bring wonderful comfort to the bereaved. Ouija boards, however, are usually a path to trouble, as practitioners tend to approach it in a spirit of fear that can draw the attention of less than high-minded spirits.

NOT-SO-NICE HAUNTS IN THE AFTERLIFE

There is a Buddhist text that describes how the Buddha overcame fear by meditating in a graveyard. Some Tibetan occult rituals involved meditation in graveyards and even practicing a special rite called *rolang,* in which a corpse was made to dance! However, these rituals are a corruption of the practices to acquire fearlessness by challenging demonical beings.

So what do you do if an evil spirit confronts you? Buddhists extend their compassion and brotherly love to all beings, including ghostly and demonic ones. According to the Lamaists, a demon does not dwell necessarily in the purgatories and can influence the earth plane as well. However, most are bound to the lower planes in the afterlife, which I will describe in detail later. The inhabitants of these gloomy worlds are beings who have been led there by their cruelty and evil deeds. Demons are beings who have made ill will a habit and rejoice in cruelty. As explained earlier, your spirituality and inner light protects you from these levels of existence, just as love and hate cannot exist in the same place. Bells, books, and candles have little effect except to increase the anxiety. If you draw comfort from wearing a religious symbol, such as a cross, crescent, Ganesh, or Star of David, it is fine, for it builds your self-confidence. Your best course, however, is to visualize yourself surrounded with loving light. Imagine God's protective energy surrounding you and you cannot be harmed.

It is usually assumed that ghosts are spirits of the dead. In many cases this is true, but there is also evidence to suggest that some ghosts emanate from the unconscious minds of living human beings. There are people who can influence matter with their thoughts and emotions. Parapsychologists call this skill *psychokinesis* (PK). For example, psychics who bend spoons or levitate objects using the mind are exhibiting psychokinetic powers. It is thought that poltergeists—ghosts that move and throw objects around—are a manifestation of this same psychic energy, which is said to be present in adolescent boys or in girls just beginning their menstrual cycles.

Some psychics say that poltergeist activity comes not from spirits or the powers of psychokinesis but from tulleric rays emitted from the earth's core. They believe that these "earth fields" can be detected by dowsing. Underground rock strata, streams, and springs distort these rays and result in areas of "geopathic stress" that are harmful to humans and some animals. At these places, the earth energy is high and poltergeist activity is likely to occur.

Dowsers also believe that the megalithic standing stones were designed to mark the lines of these earth fields. Named *ley lines* by dowser Alfred Watkins, they crisscross the world and converge on Glastonbury and Stonehenge in the United Kingdom and the pyramid of Cheops in Egypt. Studies have shown that many of the most famous cases of poltergeist activity have happened in buildings that have been built exactly on the intersection of two major ley lines.

It may be the case that poltergeist activity is not caused by spirits but by earth energies, or by living people with an extraordinarily high energy field. Returning to the Buddhist theme, it is recognized in Tibetan Bön (a form of indigenous Tibetan shamanism that was absorbed into Buddhism) that some ghosts can be deliberately created using special meditation techniques.

In particular, the meditating monk may create a Tulpa spirit that can be used, like a sort of genie, to act as the servant of the monk. Although these "beings" are only thought forms, they can occasionally run out of control and cause problems, acting in a manner similar to a poltergeist. However, if the monk ceases to meditate upon the Tulpa, its energy gradually disintegrates, and it dissolves once again into nonexistence.

Similarly, it was argued by the Spiritualist pioneer Sir Oliver Lodge that some ghosts may be a kind of mental "recording" in rooms or places where some tragedy has taken place. For example, if you go into a church, you may have a gut feeling of the atmosphere of the environment you are in. You may feel the peace and sense the spirituality of the building. This is something more than the feelings created by the stained glass and the grandiose architecture; it is a vibration of years of worship that has soaked into the very fabric of the building.

You may have had similar feelings when you decided to purchase a home. Something about the building just "feels" right— like home. Again, you are sensing the atmosphere of the place.

The same, of course, applies to places that have acquired a bad atmosphere. Imagine the vibrations present in an abattoir, or slaughterhouse. What if you were to visit a place like Belsen, a Nazi extermination camp in Germany? Even after so long, the horror of the place! Animals are very aware of vibrations. They say that, to this day, no birds sing at Belsen and Auschwitz.

An interesting experiment to demonstrate the psychic sensitivity of animals was carried out by Robert Morris of the Psychical Research Foundation of Durham, North Carolina. He put a rat, cat, dog, and rattlesnake into a house in Kentucky that was claimed to be haunted by the spirits of people who had died violently in two of the rooms.

In one of these rooms, the cat leaped onto its owner's shoulders, the dog barked, and the rattlesnake assumed an attack position. The rat showed no reaction. Perhaps, excepting the rat, the animals involved were responding to the vibrations in the place?

It may be the case that, in the time before language, we communicated with one another by telepathy (thought transference). It's possible we may have left "recordings" in the environment to warn others if a place was good or bad. Other animals may have done the same. Places such as poisoned waterholes or dangerous caves may pick up energy that would make us instinctively want to shun them.

The ability to see ghosts may be a carryover from old prehistoric skills. Not only does the seer become aware of the atmosphere of the place, but he or she also sees the actual events unfold—like a video recording in space. The truth is that not every ghost contains a conscious spirit. They may actually be no scarier than an old photograph.

A TRUE TALE OF STATELY SPOOKS

When they released the video of the movie *The House on Haunted Hill*, I was asked to help with the publicity by visiting one of Britain's most famous stately homes to see if I could prove or disprove whether it harbored any ghosts. The story is taken up by journalist Rachel Dobson in the national U.K. paper *Daily Star*:

"Recruiting the help of ghost hunter and medium, Craig Hamilton-Parker, we paid a visit to the magnificent but haunted home of the Seventh Marquis of Bath, Longleat House, near Warminster, Wiltshire.

"He's never been inside the house before and is hunting 'blind.' As Craig, who knows about these things, says joking, 'It's such a great place the spirits don't want to leave.' He looks like a friendly headmaster in his blazer and chinos, but having a chat isn't easy when there are ghosts around. He suddenly veers off down dimly lit corridors in the private quarters of the huge, echoey house, his imaginary antenna leading him to a spooky quarter.

"Standing in a bland and empty corner of the corridor, with his head bowed in concentration, Craig murmurs, 'This used to be the nursery and children would play here. But a little girl who played here with blonde, ringletted hair died of a breathing disease.'

"I stand there, not daring to breathe, the hair on the back of my neck slowly standing to attention. Craig continues: 'There's also a woman here too, but she's connected to a different time in history. I saw her standing in the corridor. A lot of tragedy has surrounded her life and she has a very ruthless husband. She's waiting for him to return.'

"I dash through the haunted area and stumble down the servants' steep spiraling staircase away from the former nursery. Down in the boiler room, when Craig senses that dead bodies have been stored on the floor, I scamper to the nearby cafe for a strong brew.

"A chat with the house steward, Ken Windess who's worked at Longleat for over 20 years, proves Craig was spot on with his ghostly sightings. In fact, baby Alice, who used to play in the nursery before it was converted into a corridor, died of consumption in 1847.

"She was exactly as Craig had described, right down to the blonde ringlets.

"As for the tragic woman, she turned out to be Louisa Carteret. Married to one of the Marquis's ancestors, she had an affair with one of the servants. Her ruthless husband found out and naturally had him disposed of. The servant was booted down the namely 'breakneck' stairs—the spiraling staircase next to the nursery—during the 1700s. His body was stored in the boiler room until it could be fully disposed of.

"Louisa was told he'd just 'gone away' and never knew he'd been bunked off. She's waiting for him, rather than her husband, in the servants' quarters where they used to meet.

"Although having ghosts around may send shivers down your spine, Craig maintains the spirits are just energies left in the air and will do you no harm."

SITTING ON LADIES' CHESTS

When you "pop your clogs" (a quaint U.K. euphemism for "kicking the bucket"), you are unlikely to bump into most of the ghosts from folklore. Sadly, you will not be able to mix with headless queens, highwaymen, gray ladies, or cavaliers. Often these supernatural characters are seen as a person awakens from dream sleep. For example, a lady wrote to me at one of my newspaper columns to say:

"I went to bed with a good book and eventually drifted off to sleep. Some hours later I awoke unable to breathe. I could see that a ghostly figure was sitting on my chest! There was an immense weight pinning me to the bed. I thought I was dying by having the breath squeezed out of my body. Somehow I managed to throw myself out of bed and staggered downstairs gulping in air as I went. I never slept there again. My unwelcome nocturnal visitor obviously objected to my presence. And I can take a hint!"

If you are planning to sit on the chests of old ladies when you enter the spirit world, think again; for this is not the result of spirits but a common complaint called *sleep apoplexy*. There's a part of the brain at the back of the head that inhibits body movement when we sleep. If it didn't, we'd act out our dreams and thrash wildly around in bed. Many people experience "sleep paralysis" when the conscious mind wakes up before this restraining function does. The result is a feeling of immobility and suffocation.

I have written for many years for a number of national papers answering people's letters about the paranormal. This phenomenon, of being pinned to the bed by a ghost, is one of the most common ones I receive. Occasionally the "ghost" does all sorts of terrible things to the person concerned. Sleep paralysis may account for many of the frightening stories we hear about ghosts and demons, which are, in effect, waking nightmares.

Fortunately, science has now identified the condition. It has been found to be very common, and extreme cases can be treated with drugs. If it happens to you, don't panic. Just relax and know that in a few moments you will wake up.

SPIRITUAL UNDERWEAR (ASTRAL SHELLS)

When we die, we shed our body in the same way we would remove our clothes. At the same time, we shed part of our astral body—the part that acts as the interface between the physical and the spiritual. This is the part that allows the spirit to use the will to move the body or make the brain function. It is not quite gross matter or spirit. I suppose we could call it our spiritual underwear.

Some mystical teachers say that, after death, the astral body separates from the physical body and also from the causal body. It becomes an "astral shell" that has no inherent consciousness of its own. It may occasionally manifest as a ghost. The Hindus call it the *Bhuta*, when it is released as a separate entity from the body and spirit. They consider it to be a devil. Indeed, some practitioners of the black arts use discarded "astral shells" as vehicles for their sorcery. Unlike the Tulpas of Tibet, which are created by intensive visualization, these entities have a material basis to them.

According to the occultist Helena Petrovna Blavatski, who founded the Theosophical Society in 1875, after death the astral body continues as a separate entity, remaining near the deserted physical body until its energy is dissipated. Occasionally, it may become visible. If she is right about this, it may mean that once you enter your spiritual state after death you would see not only your physical body but also a phantom duplicate of yourself hovering around your corpse. I would anticipate that it would be quite a hard experience seeing your own corpse, let alone meeting an astral equivalent of yourself at the same time!

Blavatski and the Theosophists also claim that mediums do not communicate with the spirits but with these astral shells that contain the memory impressions of the departed person. The enigmatic Christians take this argument a step further and claim that the astral shells are animated by demons that wish to trick us into believing we are in communication with real spirits. Their intent is to lead us away from the paths of righteousness and into hell.

But, there are a number of flaws to the arguments. First, these arguments are put forward by people who are not mediumistic and who have no direct experience of what it's like to make a communication. When the spirit links, I become aware of the whole of the spirit person. I sense the memories, the thoughts, and the feelings of love toward the recipient of the message. The evidence conveyed is often filled with humor, and it carries with it the whole weight of the human personality. This is not an animated astral shell; it is a fully functioning consciousness.

Most important, such spirit communicators can not only give evidence about their own lives but can occasionally tell us things about situations they would not have encountered when on earth. If they were just astral memory traces, they would only be able to give messages up to the point they died. However, spirit communicators know all about what has taken place since their death and will often tell the sitter what they have been doing on their way to the consultation. Similarly, why should a demon animate a spirit to bring love and comfort? Many of the people who come to me go away with their Christian faith restored and a renewed interest in actively making God part of their life.

Too much importance has been made of the astral shell—usually by those who have a vested religious interest in undermining mediumistic philosophies. It is probable that there is residue energy, but this dissipates quickly after the death of the physical body. I feel that the Chinese Taoist philosophy comes closest to the truth of the matter. According to Taoism, the spirit (soul) has two parts: yang, which is the spiritual part; and yin, which is the physical part. At physical death, the spirit (yang) leaves the body and goes to God, the yin (earthly body) returns to the earth and is no more.

THE WORLD BEYOND THE EARTH

"What happens after death is so unspeakably glorious that our imagination and feelings do not suffice to form even an approximate conception of it."

—CARL JUNG

YOUR SPIRITUAL PREPARATION

Many spiritual systems believe that life should be lived as a preparation for death. For many people, this process of spiritual preparation works on an unconscious level. Carl Jung, the famous Swiss psychologist (1875–1961), believed in a spiritual survival beyond physical death. His conviction was strengthened when he observed that dreams behaved as if the psyche will continue to exist after death. In particular, the common denominator of the dreams of the dying does not seem to be simply an end of earthly existence, but transformation into a continuing other form of life.

Jung proposed that death dreams are linked with a primordial set of archetypes and that through their analysis it is possible to conclude that life will continue after death. Jung also maintained that the belief in an afterlife means a great deal to most people and helps them to live this life more harmoniously. For those who see death as the absolute end of life, death is a great catastrophe. Those, however, who believe in eternity often regard death as a joyful event.

At many times throughout our life, dreams help us to deal with the angst of our own mortality. You may occasionally dream about death itself or dream about it even in a symbolic way. For example, a dream about death may be represented as a journey into the unknown, or as a wedding in which the soul joins its missing half with the wholeness. Gradually, such dreams can prepare your spirit for a transition that is yet years in the future.

Skeptics may argue that dreams about death and rebirth are merely expressions of wish-fulfillment. Nevertheless, dreams do reflect more than simply one's unconscious needs or wishes. Jung showed that dreams do sometimes symbolically foretell a death. They may use brutal motifs, such as clocks that stop and cannot be started again or the theme of the life-tree being hewn down. Don't be alarmed, however, if you dream about death. Such dreams often occur as a result of stress caused by relationships, job changes, money worries, and other difficulties you may be experiencing in life. Death dreams may also symbolize a life where you are becoming emotionally overwhelmed or find it hard to cope. Not all death dreams are about an actual pending death.

Jung believed that we have a "collective unconscious," which refers to the storehouse of myths and symbols that are common to all of humanity and to which everyone has access via dreams. Dreams about death and dying often draw upon this reservoir of universal ideas. Many of the images that the unconscious uses are about transformation. The Jungian psychotherapist Marie Louise Von Franz says that the dreams of those who are dying can be interpreted as preparation of the consciousness for the transformation of the psyche and its entry into the afterlife: "All of the dreams of people who are facing death indicate that the unconscious, that is, our instinct world, prepares consciousness not for a definite end but for a profound transformation and for a kind of continuation of the life process which, however, is unimaginable to everyday consciousness."

This fact was once expressed in a dream that I wrote down in my dream diary:

"I am traveling through a beautiful countryside. All around is magnificent scenery. I can hear birdsong and smell flowers. I have a deep-seated feeling of joy. Everything is alive with light. It is as if the world is made of light. I look at my hands and realize that I too am made of light.

"I come to a village hall and can hear the faint sound of voices from within. I step inside to darkness. In the gloom I can see a play in progress. Some people urge me to join in, and soon I find myself acting a part in the play. We perform one play after another. Some are tragic, others comic. I become aware that they go on forever without end."

This dream is a metaphor that expresses the human predicament. In reality, we are beings of light but have come to the world and become entwined in a series of plays. In the dream, these represent how we move from one life to another without end. Each play is another human life in which we act out our part. The problem is that we have forgotten what lies outside the village hall. We have forgotten that we are beings of light.

The Shakespearean actor Sir Ralph Richardson, who died in 1983, expressed a similar idea when he said, "The idea [of reincarnation] seems quite logical to me. Not that I think I might once have been an Egyptian pharaoh, but the idea that man, or shall we say his spirit or mind, has at one time or another in its existence inhabited some other form of body seems sensible to me. I think of life as a great pool or reservoir. We are taken from this pool and given a body, not necessarily a human body, like a suit of clothes to wear. When we have used that body to the best of our ability and it wears out, we die and for a time return to the pool of life until we are given another 'suit of clothes.'"

YOUR TRANSITION TO THE AFTERLIFE

One of the greatest joys you will experience as you enter the afterlife is the realization that bodily suffering has come to an end. When those in the spirit communicate through a medium, they often give vivid descriptions of the way they passed over and provide details of the bodily conditions they suffered at the end.

A medium will sense these conditions in his own body, although not with the full ferocity that the spirit person experienced. Considering the thousands of spirit messages I have given in my time, I have died thousands of deaths. The worst one I remember was when the spirit person "overshadowed" me with the sensation of his head being severed by a sheet of glass! It provided good evidence to the sitter, but left me with a sore throat for several days.

The new entrant to the afterlife has a feeling of exhilaration as the spirit initially leaves the body. Suddenly, all pain and discomfort are gone! We are told through mediumship that this transformation is immediate and complete. Also, spirit communicators have pointed out that the suffering when close to death is not as horrifying as it may appear. As death approaches, the body of light separates partially from the physical body so that the pain becomes distant and remote. The dying person's consciousness becomes centered on the body of light, which is free of all suffering.

Not only will all the pain be gone once you pass over, but you will also feel awash with the life force. If you die late in life, all those aches and pains of old age are wiped away in an instant. You feel free and vital. It's like being in the prime of your life—but better!

As the moment of death approaches, most people become peaceful and at ease. Although it is natural to fear death, perhaps we are all instinctively aware that there is nothing to fear. An innate knowledge that life continues comes into effect. For example, our dog William had to be put to sleep to end his suffering. Although conscious during the medical examination, William slipped into sleep as soon as the vet brought out the injection. It was as if he knew that it was his time to go, and he made the initial step into the afterlife himself. Many superstitions claim that animals know when their time has come. The most well known is the European belief that a donkey knows when it will die and hides itself away. This gives rise to the expression: "You'll never see a dead donkey"—and if you do, it's a very lucky sign.

I have no idea how I will react when my time to die comes. Like many others, I may go through stages of denial, anger, bargaining, despair, and resignation. There is no way that we can impose our own model for the ideal death. I hope that the doctors tending to me will be honest. I would personally rather know when I am to die so that I can spiritually prepare. I hope that the medication I receive will allow me to remain conscious and that the people around me will help me to continue my journey, rather than cling to my dying body. I hope that I will have courage, equanimity, and clarity, so that my spirit can focus on the experience ahead.

The 1960s hippie guru Ram Dass (Richard Alpert) tells a sad story to illustrate the conflict that the dying person may experience between the part of him that holds him to the earth and the part that wants to move on: "I was told about a twenty-eight-year-old woman named Michelle who was dying of cancer in a hospital and whose mother, a nurse in that very hospital, was working triple-time to keep her only child alive, sleeping in the next bed, leaving her side only to use the bathroom. During one of these lavatory breaks, Michelle whispered to another nurse, 'Please tell my Mom to let me go.' This wasn't possible, however, and it was not until her mother was persuaded to go out to dinner one night that Michelle managed to slip away."

Hospital patients who have had a near-death experience (NDE) report the sensation of release from suffering as they leave the body. During an NDE, the operating theater instruments show that the patient's heart stops beating, and the brain may be dead for up to two minutes. Effectively, the patient has died and then been resuscitated. Often these patients can recall with complete clarity having left their bodies and even traveling down a tunnel of light to the next world. Many of these remarkable cases have been recorded and investigated by a growing number of scientists; in particular, Dr. Raymond Moody, Dr. Michael Sabom, Dr. Karlis Osis, and Dr. Elisabeth Kübler-Ross.

It has been found that many patients, undergoing an NDE, experience the initial release from the dying body as unspeakably beautiful. There is no pain. A great majority of these people report feelings of wonder and elation. According to Dr. Kenneth Ring, sixty percent of people resuscitated describe such sensation. He quotes a subject who came close to death by drowning: "This incredible feeling of peace came over me . . . all of a sudden there was no pain, just peace. I suppose it is because it is so completely unlike anything else that I have ever experienced in my life . . . a perfectly beautiful, beautiful feeling."

Of course, loved ones left on earth are unaware of the blissful state that you experienced as you left the body. What they see is the cold, crumpled, shell left behind. The harrowing sight of your discarded body, depending on the details of your tragic demise, may remain fixed in their minds for years to come.

My father died of bone cancer—which is a cruel and debilitating illness. I watched the undertakers remove his body. As they lifted the thin, crumpled remains of this shattered shell, I thought about my own mortality and felt strangely serene that I too must die one day. Though I felt sadness, I was also supported by the innate knowledge that we are not the body. It was not my father himself they were removing. The undertakers were simply well-dressed sanitation engineers.

Naturally, many people tend to visit mediums to find out if their loved ones have made it safely to the next world. A good medium will give them this proof and reassurance. In some cases, the spirit may linger by the body for a while or need to resolve conflicts before moving on. However, in all cases this is only a short period of transition. The truth is that all people, even the bad ones, eventually make it to the afterlife, where the process of spiritual self-assessment and reconciliation begins.

THE JOURNEY TO THE NEXT WORLD

> *"The Zen master Gudo was asked, 'What happens to an enlightened man after death?' Gudo replied, 'How should I know, I haven't died yet.'"*

> —RAM DASS

❧

SINCE EARLIEST TIMES, MYTHOLOGY and religion have used allegories of a journey to represent the transition to the next life. The ancient peoples associated the death journey with the dawn of the sun and its journey across the sky. To early man the sun was immortal, as it "died" every evening, traveled through the underworld, and was "reborn" every morning. They therefore buried their dead facing the position of the rising sun and covered the bodies in red ochre to symbolize new blood and life. Confident of their rebirth, Neanderthal mourners of sixty-thousand years ago supplied their dead with the adornments, tools, and food needed when they returned. These rituals may date back to the times before our evolution into *Homo sapiens.*

The symbolism of a journey is taken up by other early religions, in particular the Ancient Egyptians. During the Old Kingdom, the sun god was Ra, who gave immortality to the collective state through the pharaoh, his son. Consequently, only the pharaoh could attain immortality, and there was no solace for the common people. Much of our understanding about their ideas comes from *The Egyptian Book of the Dead*, now accurately translated as the *Book of Going Forth by Day*. It contains a large number of funeral texts spanning the entire history of Ancient Egypt. It is a guidebook about how to behave in the afterlife, providing lots of tips to help you get a good deal. In particular, there are the stock answers and spells you will need when the god Osiris asks about your life and sins. He will weigh the deceased's heart and then judge his soul according to the good and bad deeds done on earth. The power-obsessed pharaohs took care to have a spell or two handy to ensure passing the test.

In later periods, the Egyptian hierarchy was also given these spells, and also anyone who could afford to pay for them. Provided the soul had purity of heart, it coexisted with the gods in the afterlife. The Egyptians also believed in a sort of astral double, which they called the *ka* and which was the guardian spirit, or life force. This ka looked exactly like the person and would spend time after death hovering around the tomb. They also spoke of the *ba*. Associated with the breath, or soul, this was the source animating the person. It was represented by a human-headed bird.

EGYPTIAN TECHNIQUES FOR BUYING YOUR WAY INTO HEAVEN

According to the Egyptians, the soul sets out, staff in hand, on its journey to the Osirian Field of Reeds, which is a happy place where the dead enjoy the rewards of the afterlife. It was considered to be in the general direction of the Milky Way, the Great White Nile of the sky. The soul is taken into the divine realms in the boat of the sun god, Ra, as he makes his way across the sky. The passenger disembarks in the underworld when the sun sets in the west and is taken through one of seven gates. Escorted by a jackal-headed god or a faithful dog, the soul enters the Hall of Truth and is brought forward to be judged by Osiris.

Osiris then weighs the soul against a feather. If it does not tip the scales, the soul is deemed worthy and is given entry into the Osirian Fields. However, if the heart is heavy with sin, it fails the test and is taken to a place where stern correctional treatment is meted out. In some accounts, the condemned soul is thrown into the lair of a terrible creature called *Ammit.*

The symbolism of a journey is found in mythology throughout history. The deceased is taken to the "other side" across a river, a bridge, or even on a bird's back. The symbolism of the boat dates back to the Neolithic period. The most well-known boat is that of Charon, the Greek ferryman who transports the souls of the dead across the river Styx to Hades. To this day, some people still put coins in the eyes or mouth of the dead so that they have money to pay the ferryman. And, in Europe, there is an amusing superstition that if two of these coins are removed from the corpse and dropped briefly in a glass of wine, which is afterward given to a husband or a wife, it will "blind" them to any affairs or infidelities of the other partner!

THE JOURNEY OF LIGHT

Today we still think of the transition to the afterlife as a journey. We speak of passing over, the other side, departure, going home, and so on. For example, the Incas of South America believed that the soul had to cross a bridge made of hair over a large river to reach the "silent land." Although the dreams of the dying are still filled with this ancient imagery, we no longer take the mythical stories to be fact. Instead, we talk somewhat clinically of a tunnel of light to the next world. This would appear to be a real experience that has been described in contemporary reports of near-death experiences.

Some skeptics believe that this is a hallucination caused by the release of chemicals in the brain during times of acute stress. Others say it is a memory of our birth. Another suggestion is that the experience is the result of drugs used in medication, but this is seen to be unacceptable when the matter is considered in any depth. Dr. Susan Blackmore of the University of Bristol says that the tunnel experience and the bright light are due to brain cells in the frontal lobes firing "rapidly and randomly" through a lack of oxygen. However, the tunnel effect also exists in out-of-body experiences (OBEs), where death or approaching death does not arise—and there is certainly no incidence of oxygen deprivation.

Some psychologists believe that when the brain shuts down there is a frenzy of short-lived activity in the temporal lobes. This creates the tunnel-of-light illusion that many dying people have described. You then experience a period of heightened fantasy, as opium-like chemicals are released by the brain. Your brain "tricks" you into reliving memories of loved ones and constructs a fantasy world leading you to believe that there is an afterlife. In reality, it is a figment of your imagination, created by the brain to make the process of dying more acceptable to you. Nothing but the darkness of unconsciousness follows the demise of your physical body.

What if these theorists are right? What then is there to fear? So what! You're gone. That's it for you, and humanity will continue to strive toward understanding a meaningless universe. Scientists will continue to ask "How?" while religious people ask "Why?" Yet all such questions are equally meaningless, for over the eons of time everything will return to lifeless space. All will be blissfully unaware of the futility of their existence.

Evolution was only the mathematics of DNA and served no purpose. The universe either burns itself out or becomes spread so thin that matter cannot form. The brief light of man's consciousness, wherever it may have come from, disappears for eternity. Like you, everything will be dead. Nothing will have self-awareness or awareness of existence. However, you will not suffer, or be disappointed that life is meaningless, for there will be no "you" to experience the suffering.

An alternative theory is that the tunnel experience is the result of our shift in consciousness as we move away from time and space. There's an increase of energy at the moment of death, an increase of vibrational speed. This shift is experienced as movement but is actually a change in frequency as our consciousness goes from one level of reality to another. You don't "die"; you just change your vibrational speed. The tunnel of light is the dawning of your new awareness.

THROUGH THE TUNNEL

Hallucination or not, there will be a tunnel. Once your physical body is dead, you will see a bright light appear far in the distance. You will then feel yourself drawn into the darkness, through the tunnel. You will feel yourself moving at high speed, as if you have been fired from a cannon. You shoot toward the light, perhaps at the speed of light. You hear a loud buzzing or a sound like rustling wind. You have feelings of lightness, freedom, and elation. But most important, you feel the irresistible pull of ineffable love. All fear falls away, and it is replaced by bliss.

Ahead of you, you are aware of a golden light. You tumble toward it as your new spiritual senses awaken. It is like the time of your earthly birth, when your senses were first flooded with the awareness of your new reality. Although the experience is unlike anything you have ever experienced on earth, it feels strangely familiar. You are becoming at one with your true reality. It is like waking up from a dream.

Most who have experienced this journey beyond the body say that there are no words to adequately describe it. The light you will see is . . . brighter than any earthly light and wonderfully beautiful. Although brighter than the sun, it does not harm the eyes of those who look directly into it. Many people who have returned from a near-death experience say that, as they are drawn to this light, they experience total love and acceptance.

You have encountered the formless nature of God. It is beyond description. To say it is infinite love or infinite light does not even begin to express the glory of what you experience. This is the be all and end all of everything. It is the infinite oneness. No wonder the Ancient Egyptians likened the experience of the afterlife to the sun's journey across the sky.

THE EXPERIENCE OF GOD

"All that dwells upon the earth is perishing, yet still abides the Face of thy Lord, majestic, splendid."

—THE QUR'AN

ை

THERE IS ONLY ONE GOD, but He (or She) can take many forms. The experience of the light is a merging with the infinite and unformed aspect of the godhead. I believe that, when you enter the light, you will realize the oneness of all things and have the ecstatic realization that everything is love, everything is bliss. This is our natural state as energy, as spirit beings at one with the godhead. It is the real you. However, this moment may be so fleeting that you will hardly know it has happened. For some who have already drawn close to the light during earthly life, it will be a sustained experience that can be vividly recalled. For the spiritually advanced person, it will remain as part of his or her consciousness forever. For the enlightened, it will be as if nothing has happened, for they are already at one with the infinite. Your level of spiritual attainment achieved on earth will determine your experience of the afterlife.

You have experienced the eternal.

Many NDE casebooks describe the incredible feeling of love that surrounds the journey to the afterlife. Among researcher Dr. Kenneth Ring's subjects, quoted in his book *Heading Toward Omega*, is the case of noted anthropologist Professor Patrick Gallagher, who was a complete agnostic until, at the age of 46, he had a terrible car accident in Death Valley, California. He was airlifted to Los Angeles with a badly fractured skull and other serious injuries. He was in a coma for several weeks and at one point during this time had a classic near-death experience. He realized that he was dead, and he describes how he had a joyful feeling on realizing that he was flying:

... Then I noticed that there was a dark area ahead of me and as I approached it I thought that it was some sort of tunnel and immediately, without further thought, I entered into it and then flew with an even greater sense of the joy of light ...

After what now I would imagine to be a relatively short period of time—although again time was dispensed with—I noticed a sort of circular light at a great distance which I assumed to be the end of the tunnel as I was roaring through it ... and the light—the nearest thing I can barely approximate its description to is the setting sun at the time under ideal circumstances when one can look at this object without any of the usual problems that staring at the sun causes ...

The fact is, this seemed like an incredibly illuminating sort of place, in every sense of that word, so that not only was it an awesome brightness ... with a tremendous beauty, this kind of yellowish-orange color, but it also seemed a marvelous place to be. And so this increased the sense of joy I had about this flight. And then I went through the tunnel and seemed to be in a different state. I was in different surroundings where everything seemed to be similarly illuminated by that same light, and, uh, I saw other things in it, too . . . [a] number of people . . . I saw my father there, who had been dead for some twenty-five years . . .

I also felt and saw of course that everyone was in a state of absolute compassion to everything else . . . it seemed, too, that love was the major axiom that everyone automatically followed. This produced a phenomenal feeling of emotion to me, again, in the free sense that the flight did earlier, because it made me feel that . . . there was nothing but love . . . it just seemed like the real thing, just to feel this sense of total love in every direction.

Your experiences after going through the tunnel of light are determined by your own cultural background and beliefs. In the case of Professor Gallagher, the experience of the afterlife was apparently not influenced by religious preconception, and it is more convincing by way of this fact. Many people, however, interpret this feeling of "total love" as an encounter with God.

It is not my intention here to question your personal faith or to push my own religious ideas upon you. However, there are certain qualities of God that are fundamental to all religions. All the great faiths of the world would probably agree with the fact that there is only one God and that God is omnipresent. God is also Love in its highest sense. You would probably also agree that God has an infinite dimension and can exist everywhere. God has no limits.

The differences arise when we say that our own religion is the only custodian of truth. Yet when we look without prejudice at the core teachings of all faiths, we find that they are the same. They speak the same language—the language of the heart. The multitude of religious beliefs could be likened to a pure light shining through a stained-glass window made of many colors. The source is the same but the expression is different. God is the pure light, and the colors are the faiths.

Throughout history, infinite God has manifested in many forms. Similarly, the unformed God will take form when we separate from the light. We are limited spiritual beings, so this is the only way we can comprehend what is happening to us. We will see God in a form that is in keeping with our expectations.

During the next stage of your transition, the light now appears to you as a figure. The personage is always a product of your belief and understanding of reality. For example, if you are a Christian you will most likely see Christ or an angel. If you are a Buddhist you may see a Buddha, or one of the great teachers. The Ancient Egyptian would have seen Osiris. A Hindu may see Krishna; a Moslem may see Allah in the form of the prophet Mohammed; a generic believer may see an angel (still a symbol of the spiritual realm); and some are aware only of the light. The afterlife is an inner world. It is the inner you that has survived death. Your experience now accords with your expectations. A personalized form of God gives us something understandable. There is something out there that is limited and with meaning.

HEAVEN SCENT

As you come out of the light, you will simultaneously feel the presence of God; yet also you will know that your loved ones surround you. For most people, this stage in the transition to the afterlife is experienced in an objective way. For example, you may feel that you are running across a glorious field toward a wonderful place. There in the distance you see forms you recognize as all the people you love. Sometimes a pet runs ahead and is the first to greet you. Soon you feel the embrace of those you may have lost—your mother and father, your wife or husband perhaps, and children who may have passed on before you.

You will hear the wind blowing through the trees, see light dappling the landscape, and touch the foliage. All of your familiar five senses will be involved in the experience—you may even be able to differentiate somehow the varied scents of heaven's flowers! You will have super-sensitive perceptions that are far superior to the senses of the body. For example, your eyes will not only see all things clearly, they will seem to "touch" all they encounter. The world around you will not be something remote. You will experience it as if you are "living" the world around you. As you breathe, the world will breathe. It's all you! And this realization will fill you with joy.

A point will come when you approach what might be called a border, or limit. You will feel yourself moving toward this demarcation as you experience your loved ones gathering around you and guiding you onward. The border can take many forms. You may see it as a body of water to be crossed. Perhaps you'll see a gray mist, a door, or a fence across a field. Some simply see a line. I remember one NDE account from a patient who saw her grandfather leaning across a garden gate. If she were to walk into that beautiful enchanted garden, she knew she would never have returned to earth.

At the heart of these similar experiences is the root experience that is the crossing-over point between earthly life and the life beyond. Different individuals express it in different ways. In all cases, it is an actualized representation of the transition into the next life. If you cross the threshold, you do not return.

Many NDE patients have come to this point. The accounts we have are, of course, from those who have "come back."

The first stages of your future near-death experience may have seen you desperately wishing to return to the physical body that you left somewhere "below," at the scene of your earthly demise. However, the tremendous pull of the blissful world that awaits you will draw you toward the afterlife. If this is the time for you to make your transition, the way will be opened for you, and you will experience the next phase of your heavenward journey. However, if your destiny is not complete, you will be told to return to earth. Many NDE patients who have reached this point have told us how difficult this return can be. They feel the conflict between the irresistible power of love that draws them like a magnet to the next world and the opposite pull of the earthly life and the suffering body they have left behind. In most NDE cases, it is the thought of their loved ones, children, or the spiritual work that they must still do that catapults them back into the physical body.

Dr. Raymond Moody, in his book *Life after Life*, quotes a patient who reached the transition point after her heart attack:

> As I approached more closely, I felt certain that I was going through that mist. It was such a wonderful, joyous feeling; there are just no words in human language to describe it. Yet, it wasn't my time to go through the mist, because instantly from the other side appeared my Uncle Carl, who had died many years earlier. He blocked my path, saying, "Go back. Your work on earth has not been completed. Go back now." I didn't want to go back, but I had no choice, and immediately I was back in my body. I felt that horrible pain in my chest, and I heard my little boy crying, "God, bring my mommy back to me."

It would be reassuring to think that we only go to the next world once our earthly plan is fulfilled. Perhaps there is a time determined by God when we are meant to die and nothing will postpone that fateful day. However, there must be many people who pass over the demarcation line between this world and the next without the feeling of completeness. Despite this, maybe the things we feel are important fall away and seem as nothing against the magnificence of the world ahead of us. I hope that when I stand on that threshold and know that I must leave my loved ones behind, I will have the feeling that I have done much of what I set out to do.

The thought of this situation inspires me to make the best of my life here. Life is so short. We have so little time. It is our duty to ourselves to do the things our heart knows we must do in this life—even if it means sacrificing our comfort and complacency.

YOUR LAST THOUGHTS

"Moreover, whatever state of being he remembers when he gives up the body at the end, he goes respectively to that state of being, Arjuna, transformed into that state of being."

—THE BHAGAVADGITA (8:6)

THE AFTERLIFE IS NOT A PLACE like the world you know around you now. What survives is the inner you. If you are spiritually advanced, you may skip the transition phases I described above and immediately become aware of the divine light of God. (I use the name God although I understand that this emotive word may mean different things to different readers.) Many Eastern religions believe that the last thoughts and words of the dying person will determine the level of spiritual attainment in the next life. So think twice if you find yourself in a life-and-death situation. Who knows what your afterlife prospects would be if you cry out, "Oh, shit!"

The spiritual person, at the passing moments, will think of God. As the assassin's bullets tore through Mahatma Gandhi's body on January 30, 1948, his final cry was "He Rama" (Oh, God). Clearly Gandhi was a man of exceptional spirituality, and according to the Hindu, these final words would have enabled him to merge with the godhead. Remembrance of God at the time of death leads to the attainment of this state of being. The Tibetan Buddhist will read to the dying from *The Tibetan Book of the Dead* to help them attain a fortuitous future state. By keeping the mind on God at the end of life, we draw closer to the absolute. It could be argued that the Catholic tradition of the Last Rites has a similar healing purpose, because it sets up a positive state of mind, focused on the prospect of God rather than worries about sin.

I'm sure that spiritual thoughts at the end of life will help the journey. However, saying the name of God on your last breath will not wipe the karmic slate clean, nor will a last-minute confession of your sins. The sum total of your life is what matters. The last thoughts and words do, however, reveal what your primary drive has been in life. You will carry these with you to the threshold and as you pass into the afterlife states. Someone who has habitually developed spirituality and often thinks about God is more likely to be drawn instantly to God consciousness than someone whose life has been spent on lesser things. The Eastern teachings say that a person who has followed a true sacred path in life will have greater freedom of action at the time of death. However, nothing can be done for the evil man at his dying moment, for he has no independence and is drawn forward by the weight of his past deeds.

We assume that the time of our death is something that we have no control over. However, it is said in the Eastern teachings that we only die when we have given our consent—even if this is on an unconscious level. The process may take only a fraction of a second. If death stands at your side, and you say, "No, I don't want to go. Go away!" then your death will be postponed for a while. However, there is usually a feeling somewhere in a corner of your heart that says, "It's alright."

THE COSMIC CONSCIENCE

"Those angels first inquired what my thought was, whether it was like the thought of those who die, which is usually about eternal life; and that they wished to keep my mind in that thought."
—EMANUEL SWEDENBORG (1688–1772)

WHEN WE ENTER THE AFTERLIFE, we begin a process of reviewing the life we have led on earth and assess our successes and failures. We start at the very heart of our being and gradually the self-knowledge unfolds until we understand why our life was as it was. You will start this process as you encounter what Dr. Raymond Moody has called the "Being of Light." This is an incredibly common element in accounts of near-death experiences. As I explained earlier, the abstract God takes a form according to your understanding—a Christian may see Christ, and so on.

I believe that this experience begins after a period of complete merging with God. Initially, the self-assessment happens at an abstract level of existence, before unfolding to a tangible form where you and

God appear to become separate states. In reality, we are always one with God—even now, as you read this—except we live within the illusion of separateness. The closest we can understand this first stage of the "life review" is to say that it is an inner experience—a soul-to-soul discourse within the highest state of existence.

Imagine what it is like to merge with God and to become aware that God knows everything there is to know about you. How would it feel to be so spiritually naked? What excuses could you possibly make for your misdeeds, and how would you attempt to explain away your mistakes and transgressions?

According to many NDE accounts, this encounter with a Being of Light is remarkably common. During the joining with God, there is the realization that God knows everything about you. There is a form of total telepathy between you. As the joining ceases, you will have the experience of standing before a Being of Light that may take the form of your particular understanding of what God should be like. Or God may just remain as a Being of Light, or even be invisible but with a powerful sense of nearness and reality. Again, the nature of this experience will be dictated by your own nature.

When you encounter the Being of Light you will not hear a physical voice or sounds coming from the Being, neither will the Being respond to your physical sounds. The exchange will not involve language, yours or that of any nation. There will instead be a direct, unimpeded transfer of thought, completely free of any possibility of misunderstanding. We could, perhaps, call it a heart-to-heart with God.

The subject of your initial exchange will be whether it is now your time to die. This "conversation" will not be filled with fear or angst. You will see that it is self-evident that it is your time to die, or not. You will be almost nonchalant about the fact, because you are now in tune with all strata of your being and the higher self will take precedence. All judgment is self-judgment. Almost without exception, reports from NDE cases conform to what you will say: "The Being of Light did not judge me. I judged myself."

And what could be a harder judge than our own conscience, for the conscience, in this life and the next, is the voice of God working through our higher self.

JUDGMENT DAY

"And many of them that sleep in the dust of the earth shall awake, some to everlasting life, and some to shame and everlasting contempt."

—Daniel 12:2

A GREAT MANY CULTURES believe that you will be judged in the afterlife. Many also believe that the fates of the morally good and morally bad will take a road to heaven or hell. References to the judgment of the dead can be found in the works of Plato, who mentions the judgment of the dead by three figures at the conclusion of *Gordias*. Many traditions say that you will be brought before a divine courtroom where your good and evil deeds on earth with be judged.

If you are a Moslem, you may believe that your judgment begins in the tomb. You will be visited by two angels called *Munkar* and *Nakir,* who will sit you up and ask you questions of faith. You will also be asked about the uniqueness of God and the identity of Mohammed. Get the answers correct and you will be left alone to lie in the grave until the day of the Resurrection of the Dead and the Day of Judgment. On this day you will rejoin your physical body and be assigned eternal life either in paradise or hell. It has been suggested that the first tombstones were placed on graves to keep the dead in!

Similar ideas can be found in many other Middle Eastern religions. Although the first authors of the Hebrew Bible did not teach that the human soul would survive death, there has arisen the idea that your deeds are recorded, wrongdoers will be punished, and the righteous will be resurrected. A common biblical expression for death is to go down to *she'ol*, a term taken to mean an underworld. This may be simply an expression for the grave and not a reference to an actual afterlife.

In common with Islam, the Jews believe that you have to wait for the Day of Resurrection before you will reap your reward for your good deeds. However, most Christians believe that the judgment of your soul takes place immediately after death. Depending on your righteousness you go either to heaven or to hell or, in some Christian churches, to purgatory.

Again we can find similar ideas in the East. Many people from the Far East believe that your soul will bypass the afterlife completely and the weight of your accumulated karma will decide if you are reborn on earth in good or bad circumstances. However, the ancient Vedic texts of India say that you will be judged by King Yama, who knows how to recognize liars. In Chinese Mahayana Buddhism, it is Yen-lo Wang who sits in judgment, and in Japan, it is Enma-o.

THE LIFE REVIEW

"If you develop love, you do not need to develop anything else."
—Sathya Sai Baba

❧

CLEARLY MANY OF THE BELIEFS about the judgment of the dead have been influenced by different cultural traditions. Today we are more likely to call this the "life review." This has again been reported by people who have had an NDE, and cases have been logged by researchers such as doctors Raymond Moody and Elisabeth Kübler-Ross.

The first stages of the review take place when you first encounter the Being of Light. During this stage you assess yourself from the very core of your being. However, like the many layers of an onion, you are a multidimensional being. The review takes place in your innermost self, which is at one with God, then expands to encompass the higher self and the other facets of your being. (I will explain this in more detail later.) In this next stage of the review, you know yourself as being separate from God, who now appears before you like a Being of Light or in a form that you understand to represent the godhead.

If you make the decision to die, you will now review your life. Your beliefs and cultural background will determine the form this takes. It may take place in a modern setting, or in a historical setting that conforms to your expectations. Conditions will form around you that make you feel at ease and ready to begin the long process of self-assessment.

Your entire life will be on display to you. This experience is more than memory, for you access the vibrations left in the cosmos by every event that has ever taken place. Some mystics call this the *Akashic Record*. You may experience this review as looking into a magical book that unfolds the story of your life, as if it is taking place within the pages. You may look into a crystal pool or perhaps even into a television screen. Or you may not need any imagery at all and will experience the unfolding of your life in a more abstract way. The situation that is manifested is in accordance with what makes you feel most comfortable.

Most reports from people who have had an NDE say that the inner experience is similar to memory but somehow apart from normal remembering. Some say that the memories come quickly and in chronological order. Others describe the events as happening out of sequence or all at once. Because of the nature of time in the afterlife, it is very difficult to explain the experience in earthly terms. The NDE visitor to the afterlife has only moments available in which to absorb these ineffable experiences. I would imagine that permanent new residents in the afterlife are allowed more time to become acclimated and, therefore, have a more leisurely period of assessment, perhaps punctuated with time for reflection and rest.

If you pass into the afterlife at an old age, you may have already begun the life review during the periods spent in reflection in your later years. Nowadays, we largely fear old age and spare no time thinking about the inevitable day when the Angel of Death knocks on our door. However, it is much more psychologically sound to allow some time in the latter part of life for reflection about one's life and consideration of what's to come in the hereafter. The psychologist Carl Jung said: "From the middle of life onwards, only he remains vitally alive who is ready to die with life. For in the secret hour of life's midday the parabola is reversed, death is born. The second half of life does not signify ascent, unfolding, increase, exuberance, but death, since the end is its goal. The negation of life's fulfillment is synonymous with the refusal to accept its ending. Both mean not wanting to live; not wanting to live is identical with not wanting to die. Waxing and waning making one curve."

If you have thought about the meaning and purpose of your life, then the life review will be a continuation of this process of spiritual integration. Your guardian angel will help you recall the reasons why you chose to be born and the lessons you set yourself to learn. You will then become aware of everything that has happened in your life and understand it in the context of the life plan you made. You may "see" it as a series of rapidly changing images in vibrant color. Everything will be multidimensional and moving. As each image flicks across the screen of your consciousness, it will be perceived and recognized. Scenes from your earliest childhood will seem as if they are happening at that moment. Once hazy memories will spring to life. You will have total recall—everything from the banal to the meaningful—and you will feel all the emotions and feelings associated with what you are seeing while at the same time remaining in a calm state of nonattachment.

The judgment and the life review are not a "final" event, with the application of absolute moral standards followed by purgatory, hell, or heaven. They are a starting point for further spiritual development and progression. During this period of introspection, you will discover the many capacities that need to grow in you and come up with ways to develop your spirituality.

ANGELS WITHOUT WINGS

"I looked over Jordan and what did I see? Comin' for to carry me home.
A band of angels comin' after me, Comin' for to carry me home."
—Swing Low, Sweet Chariot (AFRICAN-AMERICAN SPIRITUAL)

YOU DO NOT WALK ALONE into the next life. With you walks your greatest friend, your guardian angel who was with you when you were born into the physical world and is with you now at the end of your earthly life. Theosophists call them *devas* or *Himalayan masters*; the Indian yogis refer to their *masters*; the Christian Church speaks of *angels*; while Spiritualists refer to *guides, helpers,* and *"the gatekeeper."* Other schools of thought talk about *higher consciousness* or the *overself.* I will use the guardian angel image—although I do not personally associate this with a being with wings but as higher beings from the spirit world.

You may not know your guardian angel while on earth, but as soon as you enter the astral levels of the next world, you will immediately become aware of such a presence. You will have the comforting feeling that a divine friend is with you. Some of us are fortunate, because we get to know our guardian angel before we die. If you are mediumistic or open to spiritual forces, you may sometimes sense a guiding hand helping you through life. You may feel inspired by an outside force or may have a sense of moral guidance. At a time of great danger or despair, have you felt an angelic hand lift and shelter you from your plight? Angels are not a matter of belief but of experience.

It would be arrogant to say that the human condition is the highest level of spiritual existence. Surely there are beings that have far greater consciousness than our own. All cultures, including our own, have acknowledged the existence of spirits at levels beyond the human. We may call them angels, although many cultures call them by other names. This is one of the most fundamental themes in human spiritual and religious experience.

There are beings that have never taken earthly incarnation and also human souls that have become superhuman—closer to the angelic state than the human. Often these beings are depicted as having wings, but this is merely symbolic representation, showing that they are transcendent beings. Nonetheless, some people may see the traditional angels—wings and all—when they enter the afterlife. This is another example of our creating afterlife situations according to our beliefs. Does it matter what form the angelic world takes? In my own case, the angel guides and helpers that I am aware of take various human forms. They have told my psychic circle that they are human spirits that once walked the earth but have evolved to an angelic state and return to teach us how to be better people and grow toward spirituality. During trance, an American Indian speaks through me as well as a Tibetan monk and occasionally an Italian clown! They speak with varying levels of spiritual understanding and have occasionally given us solid proof of their reality.

Everyone has a guardian angel. Yours will be with you as you move into the afterlife and will provide a comforting influence as you progress. You may not see your spiritual friend at first, but you will have an undeniable sense that "someone" is there in the background. The angel may appear as a Being of Light, in human form, or even as an angel complete with wings. Your level of understanding and belief determines your perception. An angel may also appear to you as a mysterious figure among the crowd of family and friends who come to greet you on your arrival in the next life.

Eventually, guardian angels reveal themselves to you. As they manifest, you will realize that you have known them for eons of time. They have been with you right from the beginning. You will be deeply moved and may want to embrace them as a long-lost friend. This will be an inspiring and uplifting moment for you. You will know that you can trust this entity implicitly.

Your guardian angel will help you with the long process of assessing your life on earth. You will be touched by their love and be prepared to look at your life and hear your angel's messages about your life. As the angel speaks, the perplexing problems of your life will unfold. Why did you suffer? For what purpose were you put on earth? What did you do that was right, and what could you have done better? There will be no judgment as such, no successes or failures; you will judge yourself in the light of your spiritual understanding.

Most of us know that life is a test. It is a school where we come to learn and grow in spiritual understanding. However, the sad fact is that we stumble along in the dark not knowing what it is we are supposed to learn. If only we knew this, we would be able to break the repetitive cycles of pain that govern our life. Have you ever entered a phase of life where you say to yourself, "Oh no, not this again!" The same pattern repeats itself—it could be a relationship going wrong, a financial difficulty, or a trouble of another kind. The truth is that we didn't learn our lesson the first time around and have to repeat some of the difficult lessons we missed the last time.

Albert Einstein was once asked, "What's the most important question you can ask in life?" His reply was, "Is the universe a friendly place or not?" Your guardian angel will be able to show you that the universe is a benign place and will explain the purpose of your life. You will see why you were put into the difficult circumstances of your life and why you had to meet the people you did. Your illnesses and misfortunes will also be shown to you, and you will understand why it was necessary for these things to happen. All of this will be revealed in a spirit of great love. Angels are powerful beings and have a deep understanding about your life and your motivations. They understand intuitively and immediately. In addition they have strong wills, and as St. Thomas Aquinas said, "Their will is by nature loving." It is through this power of love that they know the secrets of your soul and will give you the joyful guidance and wisdom you need in order to assess yourself.

The people we love in the spirit are able to see how much we suffer in this world and how unnecessary much of our grief is. Earth is a dark place, where ignorance reigns supreme. But it is changing. Many spiritual beings have incarnated to help us reestablish truth and light in this world. The spirit people tell us that we are on the threshold of a golden age. From the blissful world of the afterlife, they are helping the process of creation to unfold. They are encouraging us to drive out the darkness, ignorance, superstition, violence, and selfishness that plague this world. Their task is to bring sublime knowledge of the purpose of human life . . . in this world and in the next.

The life-review process at this newly arrived stage is a continuation of the initial rapid period of self-assessment you made when you encountered the godhead. The process continues as you begin to understand and integrate life's lessons. People who have encountered the initial stages of the life review, through an NDE, have a remarkable agreement about the nature of these lessons. Some have spoken of the importance of seeking knowledge, but invariably they stress the importance in this life of trying to cultivate love for others. The goal of human evolution is to attain the higher consciousness that can best be described as love—but even this word cannot express this ineffable state of bliss. You will judge yourself according to your capacity to love.

TALKING TO YOUR SPIRIT GUIDE

Although there is no problem recognizing guardian angels as soon as you see them in the afterlife, it is also possible to make a connection with them before we die. Part of their mission is to help and guide us in our earthly life.

Mediums become familiar with their guardian angel, in Spiritualist circles often called the *gatekeeper* or *doorkeeper*. This is your main spiritual helper, who sees you into this life and guides you through the next. However, we also gather other spirit "guides" and "helpers" around us who can help with spirit communication and protect the medium from negative influences. In the medium's case these guides may help with specific tasks such as healing, work with child spirits, clearing negative energies, and so on. In my own work, I have an American Indian as my "guardian angel/gatekeeper," a Tibetan as my "trace control," and an Italian clown who helps me with my public demonstrations of mediumship. There are others, too, who work in the background of my awareness.

Guiding History

Non-mediumistic people may also have spirit guides and helpers working through them. These are often people you know who have gone over to the spirit and do the work—a dead relative or someone known very well in this life may serve as a guide. Many great men and women have accredited their genius to the guidance received from spiritual influences. For example, the pianist Liberace believed that, at times, he was paranormally inspired. He owned the piano that once belonged to the classical composer Franz Liszt. "When I play his compositions on it, I have the most eerie feeling, as if I'd played that music before in another time," he said. And just like Liberace, Lizst was a flamboyant dresser.

Lucille Ball believed that she received help from the dead actress Carole Lombard. Jayne Mansfield also received spirit guidance: "The woman I admire most, Ethel Barrymore," she said, "spoke to me. Then my Aunt Kathy, who had been dead these fifteen years, talked to me and her voice was exactly as I remembered it. Aunt Kathy always had a great sense of humor. She still has." Ms. Mansfield also held séances in Rudolph Valentino's former home, Falcon Lair, and received guidance from the "dead" silent-screen legend.

Sports men and women have also said that they sometimes feel guided by the spirits. Donald Campbell, the former British car and speedboat racer, believed in life after death. He spoke on a number of occasions of feeling the presence of his dead father, Sir Malcolm Campbell, with him in the cockpit of his boats and rocket cars. As he sat in the cockpit of the *Bluebird* and prepared to achieve his 648 kph (403 mph) land-speed record on Lake Eyre salt flats, Australia, he saw his father's spirit. "He was crystal clear and looked down at me with the half-smile on his face I knew so well," wrote Campbell.

Then he heard the spirit say, "Well, boy, now you know how I felt on the morning of September 2 at Utah in 1935"—the day his father burst a tire at over 480 kph (300 mph). His father's voice encouraged Donald Campbell. Like his father before him, Donald became holder of both the water- and land-speed records.

Perhaps one of the most intriguing comments about spirit guides was made by Sir Winston Churchill, who said, "I have a feeling that we have a guardian because we serve a great cause and that we shall have that guardian so long as we serve that cause faithfully."

Exercise: How to Connect with Your Spirit Guide

In his book *The Life Beyond Death*, Arthur Ford wrote "I am convinced that becoming aware of the next stage of existence beyond the earth biosphere is very largely a matter of becoming attuned to its vibrations." If you are sincere and attempt to raise your consciousness through regular meditation, you are likely to feel the invisible presence of your spirit guide. Many people find this an exciting experience, but it is important to remember that it is a normal part of your spiritual development. Just because you have made contact with your guide/angel does not mean that you are in any way unique, or chosen for a special destiny. It is important to remain modest and keep your feet firmly on the ground. It is also advisable to avoid "guide worship." The guides that help us with our life are spiritually advanced beings but, like us, have limitations.

It is spiritually beneficial for you to establish a communication in this life, for this will help you to accelerate your spiritual advancement as well as prepare you for the life to come. It may take many years to develop a full rapport with your guide/angel. This is best accomplished by sitting in regular meditation with like-minded people with a similar intent. What is particularly helpful is a medium who can guide your group. Unfortunately, it is now difficult to find good teaching mediums, but this method will get you started on your journey to spiritual understanding.

STEP 1. You need to establish a regular time to sit for meditation in order to attune yourself to your guide/angel. The guide/angel is also eager to establish a connection and needs to know when to draw close. Self-discipline is important so that the guide only draws close when he/she is invited to do so. A regular time for attunement helps both sides to achieve a blending of consciousness.

Step 2. Sit upright in a comfortable chair, and let go of all stress, allowing yourself to slip into a deeply relaxed state. As you become more relaxed, you will notice your breathing slowing down. Let the warm feeling of relaxation spread upward from your toes and feet until your whole body is completely relaxed.

Step 3. Once you are completely relaxed, you will notice that your mind is slowing down. For a while just enjoy being in this comfortable state. You are totally relaxed, yet remain alert and awake.

Step 4. Spirit guides are able to influence your consciousness when your mind is quiet and still. This allows them to align their rate of vibration with your own. Within this stillness, you will become aware of the gentle, loving vibrations of your guide. At no time are you in any danger, and you are always in complete control. You are establishing a spirit-to-spirit communication and at no stage can the guide, or anything else for that matter, take you over.

Step 5. During this state, you may have a glimpse of someone who was known to you and who loved you, such as a wife, husband, or parent. These clairvoyant visions may make you feel happy and inspired. Be encouraged if you see swirling colors or visions from your own mind, as this shows that your mind is opening to new ideas and inspiration. Also, be aware that not everybody "sees" the spirit people. It is fully as valid to inwardly "hear" or "feel" your spirit guides.

Step 6. Pay close attention to everything you experience during meditation. The thought processes you are having will help to strengthen the link between you and the spirit world. You may also discover that this technique increases your ability to communicate telepathically with people in this world as well as in the next.

96

Step 7. It is most important to realize that what is happening is real. You are being given guidance from intelligent spirit people who have been charged with helping you. Broaden the bridge between you by inwardly thanking them when you believe that you have been given a glimpse of your guide/angel or have intuitively received some helpful information. Your thoughts are potent forces that go out from you and influence the world. They will be received by those in the spirit—even if you are not aware that they have "heard" you.

Step 8. Be patient. Do not bombard your guide/angel with a stream of requests. You may, of course, ask the occasional question, but the answer may not always come immediately. You will get a reply when you are ready to receive it. You will not be receptive while you are straining your intellect, reaching for the expected answer. Your answer may come through during meditation or during a later period of reflection. It may be given to you coincidentally, such as an overheard conversation, or something you read in a book. Know that you will be guided.

Step 9. Discovering the identity of your guide/angel is not of primary importance. It does not matter whether your guide was a great saint, philosopher, pauper, or king. What matters is the quality of the spirit person who is helping you. It is often the most humble people who live the most spiritual lives. Do remember, however, that even though they are part of a hierarchy of angelic beings dedicated to helping people who have a spiritual intent, these guiding spirits are limited beings, like us.

Step 10. Your most important insights will come in the form of a silent influence, as these spiritual beings blend with your own character and thought. They will help you overcome your negative traits, inspire you in times of crisis, help you rid yourself of selfishness, and enable you to become a better person. Intervention by angels, throughout time, has been accepted as an important part of most religions. It is still happening today.

READY, OR NOT

"We receive, day after day, the misfits, the derelicts, the outcasts, the flotsam and jetsam, the millions who come here unprepared, unready, unequipped, and who have to learn all over again. Instead of passing to our world a stream of evolved souls ready to take up the tasks that await them, there come millions who have to be treated and nursed and tended because they are bruised, like little children."

—Silver Birch (American Indian guide of journalist Maurice Barbanell)

❧

Modern man has a dilemma with death and shrinks from the dark thoughts of approaching old age. Fathers wish to be brothers to their sons and mothers to be sisters to their daughters. There is no dignity in old age, and society encourages us to cling to our fading youth. Just as a childish person shrinks away from the unknown in the world and in human existence, so the maturing person shrinks back from the latter part of life. No longer do we look to our senior citizens for wisdom, but consider old age as being some form of malady. A materialistic age places little value on the special spirituality that can only come from experience and reflection.

A human life is like the arc of the sun as it crosses the sky. The first quarter, lying to the east, is childhood. As the sun rises to its zenith it becomes brighter, symbolizing the expansion of our consciousness and its expression in the world. However, as it descends, the light of the sun returns into itself before its journey through the underworld. Similarly, the latter part of our life can become a period of introspection as the light of our consciousness returns to within itself. Perhaps we could learn from ancient times when the aged were the custodians of secrets and the seers of visions. The life review can begin at this time . . . and continue after death.

Contemplation of the afterlife, at any stage in life, will prepare you for crossing the threshold without fear. An awareness of your guardian angel and proof of the reality of the next world from mediumship can reinforce this spiritual readiness. However, there are a great many people who never think about what's to come and are spiritually unready to make the transition. (I have already spoken of what can happen if a person clings to the earth plane or is unaware he or she is dead.) The life review—described earlier—is merely the initial stage of your gradual familiarization with your new world. Your emotional and spiritual state at the time of death will determine how long a period of self-assessment you need. If you are spiritually unready, then your spiritual self-improvement may take a great deal of time—indeed, the afterlife is not a static place but is full of activity.

SUICIDE

"Trust me, trust in our love. You will learn and grow through my
death. You will know it was my path and destiny to end my life
in that moment. It was my life's lesson. What I've now given
you is a tiny molecule of the lessons I've learned since death.
My suicide is also connected to a greater good. You will see it, in
part, unfold in your own life."

-ALBERT FLEITES (FROM THE SPIRIT WORLD TO JOEL
ROTHSCHILD)

❧

SUICIDE IS PERHAPS THE worst instance of being spiritually unprepared for death. Some pretty horrible punishments have been imagined by religions for those who take this road. For example, in the fourteenth century, Dante Alighieri published the famous epic poem called the *Divine Comedy* and claimed to have visited hell and purgatory. In the lower depths was found the forest of suicides. Here, the souls of those warped by the sin of self-murder were transformed into grotesque trees. Because they rejected life on earth, they now stood fixed and withered in hell.

Dante's description of the fate of people who had committed suicide was not confirmed by the work of mediums. For example, twenty-one-year-old Rob Willis suffered from clinical depression. On May 12, 1999, he could take no more and killed himself by throwing himself off a multistory parking garage. His mother, Jean Willis, was devastated when the police knocked at her door after midnight to tell her the terrible news.

"Inside, I started to scream," said Jean, when she spoke about her loss in a newspaper article about mediumship. "My only child. I was divorced and we'd been so close. I knew he'd been depressed.

But suicide? How could he? The terrible news was so upsetting that, in the days ahead, I, too, seriously contemplated suicide. I just wanted to be with Rob.

"One lunchtime, five weeks after his death, I was surfing the Net and came across Craig Hamilton-Parker's website. I booked a consultation and the first thing Craig said to me was that he felt a young man called Rob was close. Then he said that he felt a sensation of falling from a great height and cars were nearby. Craig confirmed that Rob had taken his own life. I was amazed. All of this before I had even said a word.

"Then Craig told me lots of factual information about Rob. He spoke about our Christmas holiday in China. Our trip to Indonesia. Even the names of the family cats, Brian and Floss. He also mentioned two friends of Rob's, Si and Nick.

"Craig said that Rob was wearing a cowboy hat. This was one of the few items of clothes I had of his—we'd bought it while on holiday. Then Craig said: 'We must never use the M word.' I gasped. This was a private joke between Rob and me about whether or not I should get married again.

"Through Craig, Rob explained to me that my suicide would be pointless. I could not join him that way. I had to be here on earth to help others."

Since the above consultation and newspaper article, Jean has joined my mediumistic development circle and has had many communications from Rob. Some of this has come from my fledgling mediums and also direct from Rob while I am in trance. His communications have given us some direct insight into what happens to people who commit suicide.

The most important thing suicide cases wish to tell us is that they are definitely not punished—at least not in the sense of being turned into trees or thrown into limbo or a pit of hell! The guardian angels quickly draw close to these unprepared souls and a process of healing begins. There is a certain amount of self-punishment, as the person is gradually made to confront what he or she has done, but this is a matter of guilt and shame rather than retribution. Once suicides are free of the earthly problem and now transcend their despair, they become aware of how much they have thrown away.

Rob has told us that he came to understand that taking his own life was a foolish thing to do. He also appears to understand, however, that for him there are karmic reasons for why it had to be. Nonetheless, he is now working to make up for the wrong he has done. He is helped by his mother, Jean, who is now developing into a first-class medium and is especially concerned with helping other mothers who have lost their children. It has been shown to us that Rob is working very hard, from the other side, to help Jean maintain the high level of evidential mediumship she has attained.

In traditions such as Tibetan Buddhism, there are specific rituals that are designed to help the soul immediately after death to move through the *bardos* and to its next incarnation. Similarly, in her own way, Jean helped her son to progress by holding him in her heart and by talking to him. Now Jean has had proof that Rob has not only survived death but is actively helping his mother. Her son has become her spirit guide.

I have come to understand that the most important power in this universe is the power of love. If a person's heart is filled with sincere love, it can build a bridge of light to the next world. Love is the eternal force that can shatter even the strength of iron or steel. Nothing can stand in its way, not even death. Mediumship would be impossible without it.

COSMIC SLEEP AND HEALING

"As well-spent day brings happy sleep, so life well lived brings happy death."

—Leonardo da Vinci

༄

Rob is one of many who take their own lives but come back to reassure their loved ones that they are safe and well. It is remarkable that he was able to communicate just five weeks after his death. Normally, with such tragic cases, the newly arrived in spirit needs time to recover from the ordeal and spends some time in a healing sleep.

There are some mediums who say that everyone "sleeps" when they enter the spirit world, and that it is impossible to communicate with the deceased until some time has passed after the death. I have not found this to be the case. There have been instances where the spirit has been able to give a clear evidential message almost immediately upon entering the spirit world. For example, I remember giving a detailed message at a Spiritualist church from someone's father. He was an amusing man and was joking about the fact that he was dead. His concluding message was, "Tell her that I am lying on a marble slab being shaved as we speak." The lady in the audience confirmed that the funeral was to be the next day and the mortician was at that moment preparing the body.

But many spirits definitely need to sleep and undergo a healing process when they arrive in the afterlife. A good friend of mine took his life in a terrible way, by covering himself in gasoline and then lighting a match. He went up like a human torch and died slowly in dreadful agony. He also died alone in a hospital, as he had nothing on him to identify him. I found out later that they had even made an announcement nationally on television news, hoping to find someone who knew who he was. My friend took his life because he had a mild form of schizophrenia that ran out of control when he took LSD. For him, fire was a form of cleansing.

God only knows what mental state he was in when he arrived in the afterlife.

Some years later, my dead friend spoke to me through a medium. The medium's face went bright red as he explained that he was feeling colossal heat as the spirit linked with him. My friend was able to give good evidence to prove who he was and went on to describe what happened to him when he entered the afterlife.

The spirit told me that he went to an area of the afterlife that some have called the *halls of healing* or the *home of rest.* This is a sort of heavenly hospital where souls who have been damaged can be brought back to wholeness. If you had a violent passing, were suffering from shock, or had a lingering illness, you will spend some time here before moving on into the afterlife.

Some of the spirits who speak through mediums tell us that, when they first entered the spirit world, they continued doing what they were doing immediately before they passed over. For example, one told us that he was run over as he crossed the road. His death was immediate and instantaneous. His spirit, however, kept on walking as if nothing had happened at all! For a while, the reality he was accustomed to around him had been maintained. For him, the afterlife included streets, shops, cars, hot-dog stands, and laundromats.

The spirit communicators who have spoken through my own trance mediumship, and also through many thousands of other mediums before me, have told us that there are many planes in the afterlife and that many of these are inconceivable to anyone living on earth. However, they have also told us that the individual survives death in a form not unlike his present mode of being. Your experience of "reality"—particularly in the initial phases of your transition to the next world—will be very similar in nature to the one you know now. For example, you will live in a three-dimensional world, and time will move forward from past to present. You will experience your surroundings in a way similar to the way you use your five senses now. Communications from the dead also suggest that you will lead a purposeful existence. In fact, there is a feeling of being more "alive" than we are.

Much of what my friend said through the medium conforms to the ideas of Spiritualists and in particular with the writings of Anthony Borgia. His books were communicated to him via mediumship from 1909 onward from a spirit person called Monsignor Robert Hugh Benson, a son of Edward White Benson, former archbishop of Canterbury. In Borgia's book *Life in the World Unseen,* the spirit communicators describe the halls of healing as being a "stately building set among well-wooded grounds." Within this building are various areas for different types of recovery. For example, there are special halls for people who have had a violent death, and so on. Borgia also tells how healers wear their spirit robes, whereas new visitors to the afterlife are dressed in clothing similar to their earthly ones.

According to Borgia, as you enter the healing halls you are surrounded by a blue ray of light that gives you a feeling of tranquility and simultaneously energizes your spirit. You may feel the light as a warmth that gently soothes your pains away. Any stress that you have carried forward into the next life is washed from you. You will begin to feel strong and well.

When you are taken into this place, you will fall into a state of absolute rest similar to what we may describe as sleep. During this time there are no unpleasant dreams, or fevers, or delirium. Your soul is at one with "divine providence" and undergoes a process of healing. Many other mediums and healers have described a similar scene. For example, the world-famous spiritual healer Harry Edwards writes of how the "place of healing" has a circle of brown stone seats and the building itself is made of a strange blue stone. The contemporary medium James Van Praagh makes a similar observation, saying, "The buildings seemed to be made of jewel-like substances, like mother of pearl and diamond. All the colors shone and blended in perfect harmony. The more I stared at these buildings, the more I realized the type of tasks being done in each individual structure."

Borgia describes the residents of the halls of healing as resting upon couches. Other accounts, such as one by occultist Yogi Ramacharaka, compare this slumber of souls to being again in a womb, preparing for another birth. A wistful feeling comes when souls understand that they have, in getting to this stage, fulfilled a part of their destiny. They also experience a sense of satisfaction as they approach this period of recuperation. According to Ramacharaka, the more advanced spiritual person requires a longer period of sleep, just as the higher animals tend to have a longer gestation and period of birth on the material plane. He points out that this is not a place but a "condition" or a "state." The situation is such that no malign or harmful influence could reach or draw near those in this state of being.

MESSAGES FROM HOME

During your period of recuperation from the traumas of earthly life, you may become aware of thoughts and feelings being projected to you from earth, perhaps of those who mourn for you. It is a help to you when your relations and friends in the earthly plane think of you with love and affection. You will not be harmed by their feelings of grief at your passing, as these, too, are expressions of their love for you. But the vibrations that will warm you the most, and best help you to adjust to your new state of being, are those that arise from positive thoughts and feelings. People on earth who remember or think about you with love, without weeping and distorted passion, will further your progress.

We can draw lessons from this now. Thoughts of goodwill projected to those you love in the next world will help them. But sorrow and longing for the departed soul delays its entry into the halls of healing. When someone you love dies, send them feelings of joy and encouragement. Dark thoughts only act as obstacles to the joy that awaits them.

RECALLING YOUR PAST LIVES

The cosmic sleep helps to restore the vitality of your spirit body and increases its light. Cosmic sleep is also part of the integration process into the next world. Just as we "sleep on it" in this life when we are making decisions or solving problems on earth, so too do we use this same method in the next life. We will go through some of the life review with our guides and helpers then spend a little time after each session in cosmic sleep. This is part of the spiritual integration. You may need a lot of cosmic sleep, or none at all—it all depends on the level of spiritual advancement you attained in earthly life.

Eventually, you will be shown beyond the immediate issues of the life you have just left and will see your situation relative to the many lives you have lived on earth before. Many of the things that have happened in this past life will be seen to be a result of karma brought forward from previous lives. For example, you may have many relationship problems in this life because you were a cheat in an earlier life. Similarly, you may have money problems in this life because you were miserly in another life. By examining your life in this context, you will gradually be shown the main lessons you should have learned from this life. An intriguing account of the judgment of the dead, which was witnessed by Dr. John Hislop and recorded by Dr. Samuel Sandweiss, was given by an elderly American, Walter Cowan, who died suddenly on Christmas Day in 1971 from a heart attack.

Walter Cowan's body was taken by ambulance to a hospital, where he was certified dead. During his life, Cowan was a devotee of the Indian holy man called Sathya Sai Baba. His wife prayed to Sai Baba for her husband to be brought back from the dead. Eventually Sai Baba agreed and interrupted Cowan's life review:

"Then Baba took me to a very large hall where there were hundreds of people milling around. This was the hall where the records of all my previous lives were kept. Baba and I stood before the Court of Justice. The person in charge knew Baba very well, and he asked for the records of all my lives. He was very kind, and I had the feeling that whatever was decided would be the best for my soul."

Walter Cowan then explains how the angels brought in many scrolls written in many ancient languages. Sai Baba examines them and makes some comments. The scrolls are the history of Cowan's past lives: "When they reached the time of King David, the reading of my lives became more exciting. I could hardly believe how great I apparently was in each life that followed. As the reading of my lives continued, it seemed that what really counted were my motives and character, as I had stood for outstanding peaceful, spiritual, and political activity . . .

"After about two hours, they finished reading the scrolls, and the Lord, Sai Baba, said that I had not completed the work that I was born to do and asked the judge that I be turned over to him to complete my mission of spreading the truth. He requested that my soul be returned to my body under his grace. The judge said, 'So be it.'

"The case was dismissed and I left with Baba to return to my body. I hesitated to leave this wonderful bliss. I looked at my body and thought it would be like stepping into a cesspool to return to it, but I knew that it was best to complete my mission so that I could eventually merge with the Lord, Sai Baba. So I stepped back into my body . . . [and] that very instant it started all over again—trying to get my breath, being as sick as you could be and still be alive. I opened my eyes and looked at my wife and said, 'You sure look beautiful in pink . . . '"

CARL JUNG'S EXPERIENCE OF THE LIFE REVIEW

I have occasionally quoted psychologist Carl Jung's views of the afterlife and the fact that the psyche appears to prepare the dying person for an entry into a new life. Toward the end of his life, Jung had a number of visions of the afterlife that also suggest that part of the life review is concerned with an examination of a person's past lives. At the beginning of 1944, Jung was taken into a hospital and experienced "deliriums and visions" as he hovered close to death. He explains encountering a "tremendous dark stone block, like a meteorite. It was about the size of my house, or even bigger. It was floating in space, and I myself was floating in space."

The immense rock had been carved into a temple, with a black Hindu sitting guard at the entrance. As Jung stepped inside this temple, he felt that everything about his earthly life was falling away from him. He had a feeling that, now, he would understand the mystery of his life. But something interrupted him:

"From below, from the direction of Europe, an image floated up. It was my doctor, Dr. H—or rather, his likeness—framed by a golden chain or a golden laurel wreath. I knew at once: 'Aha, this is my doctor, of course, the one who has been treating me. But now he is coming in his primal form, as a basileus of Kos. In life he was an avatar of this basileus, the temporal embodiment of the primal form, which has existed from the beginning. Now he is appearing in that primal form.'

"Presumably, I too was in my primal form, though this was something I did not observe but simply took for granted. As he stood before me, a mute exchange of thought took place between us. Dr. H had been delegated by the earth to deliver a message to me, to tell me that there was a protest against my going away. I had no right to leave earth and must return. The moment I heard that, the vision ceased."

When Jung eventually returned to waking consciousness he was very concerned for the welfare of Dr. H. He pleaded with his nurses to warn him. "His life is in danger, for heaven's sake! He has appeared to me in his primal form! When anybody attains this form it means he is going to die, for already he belongs to the 'greater company'!"

Carl Jung was Dr. H's last patient. On April 4, 1944, Jung was allowed to sit up on the edge of his bed for the first time since the beginning of his illness. On the same day, Dr. H took to his bed and eventually died of septicemia.

My own spirit guide, Taratha, has spoken about the primal form, which we attain once we have become fully integrated into the afterlife. As far as I understand, this is what others have called the "overself," the highest aspect of our consciousness. Taratha has also told my circle that only a fraction of our self incarnates on the earth at any one time. We are like a many-faceted diamond of which only one surface is in this world at any one time. The primal self is the core personality that has lived many times before and that is fully aware of the purpose of its existence in past lives, this life, and the lives to come.

It is the real you.

THE FIRST STATES AFTER DEATH

Earlier I described the halls of healing as both a "state" and as a "place." So which is it? Do we enter abstract forms of being when we go to the afterlife, or does it have places similar to those we know in earthly life? I have begun to address some of these questions earlier in this book, but now would be a good time to look at this in more detail, before we continue our journey in the afterlife itself.

Life in the afterlife is, I believe, similar to the world many people experience during what psychologists have called "lucid dreaming." During lucid dreaming the sleeper "wakes up" while the dream is taking place and discovers that he or she can change the dream at will. Lucid dreams are extraordinarily vivid, and the colors and forms can be more "real" than waking life. They are much more realistic and consistent than most dreams. As you have a great deal of conscious control over the dream, it means that you can do pretty well anything you like. For example, in a lucid dream you may be able to fly, or run at great speed, or you can create landscapes and use your imagination to perform extraordinary feats of creativity. Somehow, the "whole" of your brain kicks into gear, and a simple creative idea will unfold spontaneously into magnificent landscapes and panoramas. During lucid dreams, you may see some extraordinarily beautiful things.

Now, imagine what it would be like if you could enter this state of consciousness not during sleep, but while fully awake. Could life in the afterlife be like this?

When we have an ordinary dream, we may dream of doing

things such as walking down the street. In your dream, you will be aware of the scenery around you and will have a body just as in waking life. You will feel your legs moving, may hear sounds and even smell things. The dream situation will be very much like normal everyday life. However, your physical body is doing nothing at all. It is in bed. Although we take it for granted, the body in which we find ourselves in dreams is not our real body. All the experiences take place in another body, which can be referred to as the *dream body.*

Some people have trained themselves to have regular lucid dreams and deliberately exploit them. The world they experience in lucid dreams is as real as the one they know in waking life. It may be the case that some of these dreams take place in the spirit body, as several people have visited their own bedroom during a lucid dream and seen themselves asleep in bed.

Life in the afterlife may be a little like an extraordinary lucid dream.

LUCID DREAMS AND OUT-OF-BODY EXPERIENCES

Some of the most important work in this area of research was done by Robert A. Monroe (1916–1995). Monroe was a regular lucid dreamer and had many out-of-body experiences (OBEs). In the mid-1950s, he set up his own foundation, the Monroe Institute, to try to understand his experiences. In particular, he invented a technology called *hemi-sync,* which consisted of feeding sound into the two hemispheres of the brain to facilitate altered states of consciousness—especially OBEs.

Monroe claimed that, during his lucid dreams and OBEs, he was put in touch with the afterlife. He spoke of his contacts with benevolent nonphysical entities whom he called *inspecs,* short for "intelligent species." He recounted his journey to the year 3500.

He told of beneficial contacts with his former lives, all of these lives existing simultaneously in the parallel dimensions he visited. (Monroe discovered that his favorite inspec guide was himself!—from his own future, now his present. He learned, close to the end of his life, that it was he who would conduct the conversations with himself that helped him, forty years earlier, to first navigate other dimensions of our universe.)

Many of Monroe's experiences follow ideas similar to those of the Spiritualists, except that they are interpreted with perhaps a more modern slant and modern-sounding names. For example, Monroe speaks of the "I-there," which is much the same as the life record revealed in the "life review" described earlier. The "I-there" is a place where everything we have ever experienced in all our lives, in this and every other dimension, is gathered together to help us through our individual lives.

Monroe journeys to a place in the next world that he calls *focus 23*. It is here that confused spirits of the newly dead gather in order to orientate themselves. Monroe next comes upon a place that is similar to the halls of healing and which he describes as a park. Spirits are brought here to rest and prepare themselves for the next step. He calls this *focus 27*. Monroe claims that in the Lifeline Program at his institute, he has trained hundreds of people to help guide the dead to that focus 27 park. Lying in tiny cubicles in darkness and wearing earphones, his students are able to leave their bodies and embark on their out-of-body journeys, communicate with inspecs, and guide lost souls to the park. (This is very similar to what some Spiritualist circles do in "rescue circles.")

But is it all just fantasy? Probably not, for in a number of cases Monroe's voyagers beyond the physical have been able to obtain names, addresses, and other information about the spirits of the dead whom they have helped. Monroe has been able to search out corroboration.

Most of Monroe's ideas are similar in essence to the classic descriptions of the afterlife from sources such as Spiritualism, Spiritism, and the philosopher Swedenborg. However, Monroe places these ideas in a modern context and, most important, shows how it is possible to use lucid techniques to communicate with these realms. Perhaps future research will show that lucid dreams are a practical method to investigating the afterlife, because the lucid dream state and the state of consciousness after death are very similar.

The similarity of the after-death state and lucid dreams explains why different people describe the afterlife in different ways: the kinds of dreams we have depend on our memories, fears, hopes, desires, and beliefs. And just as dreams reflect our personalities and waking beliefs, so the world we enter after death depends on what we have done and believed while alive in the physical body.

Because of this, many people will continue to experience a dreamlike continuation of their life . . . before death. The Swedish visionary philosopher Emanuel Swedenborg (1688–1772) describes this first state after death:

"The first state of man after death is like his state in the world, because he is still in like manner in externals. He has therefore a similar face, similar speech, and a similar disposition, thus a similar moral and civil life; so that he knows no other than that he is still in the world, unless he pays attention to the things that he meets with, and to what was said to him by the angels when he was raised up—that he is now a spirit. Thus one life is continued into the other, and death is only the passage."

Imagine what sort of afterlife the surrealist painter Salvador Dali would experience. Some people may undergo the most fantastic adventures and see worlds and places that are incomprehensible to us now. Others may suffer from recurrent nightmares, trapped in some form of hell that has been created by their own minds. (Swedenborg and many great mediums such as Andrew Jackson Davis have emphasized that man must do penance in the afterlife for sins committed in this one, but that there is no hell as such.) There will also be many who will experience an afterlife that is completely in accordance with their spiritual or religious background. For example, a Catholic may meet St. Peter by the "pearly gates," and a Moslem may see the green gardens described in Islamic literature. Normal dreams are a very personal experience, but there is evidence to suggest that it is possible for telepathy to take place in dreams. From my newspaper columns and Internet site, I have received many letters over the years from people who claim to have shared the same dream as someone close to them, or spoken to each other through a dream.

Your afterlife state will not be confined to personal fantasy, because there will be a clear telepathic link between your own inner world and that of other people you meet. Although you are sharing thoughts, you may sometimes choose to use language. You will also have "dreams" in common. For example, when you meet someone you knew well in life, you may generate a scene that you can both share, such as a happy place that you remember from the earth plane. This process will be spontaneous and automatic.

Dreams may also be able to take on a life of their own. Many of the early Spiritualists believed that the spirit world has an almost "physical" reality. During séances, the early Spiritualists would see a smoke-like substance called *ectoplasm* exude from their mediums and build into seemingly solid forms of spirit people. During these incredible séances, the sitters saw their loved ones as being solid and could even touch them. It was theorized that ectoplasm is a substance that is neither material nor spiritual, but a material that could bridge the two worlds. In our world, energy vibrates at a slow speed to create matter. However, material in the spirit world is a form of matter with energy that vibrates at a much higher rate. Ectoplasm falls somewhere between the two. The "matter" of the spirit dimension has a similar physical reality but can be manipulated by the mind. The environment of the spirit world is, therefore, a solid reality created from the collective thoughts of humanity.

In *The Unfolding Universe*, the Spiritualist pioneer Arthur Findlay describes it thus: "Etheria, however, is the name for seven worlds, one within the other, and if we include the earth there are eight. These eight worlds or globes, one inside the other, resemble a wooden ball I have seen which can be unscrewed but only the outer ball or surface comes away from the rest, as underneath the outer ball is another, and so on till we come to a small one inside the rest. This last ball can be compared to our earth. Each of these worlds has a surface, an atmosphere and light, so what I say of one refers to all. It must not, however, be assumed that the places where we have mountains and seas on earth have corresponding mountains and seas just above them in Etheria. The forces which made mountains, land and sea on earth, likewise made them in Etheria, but not necessarily in the self-same locality as they are on earth."

A clear explanation was given through the mediumship of Mrs. Leonard during a séance with the great physicist Sir Oliver Lodge, who received many messages from his dead son Raymond. "You live in a world of illusions," said Raymond, "illusions necessary to enable you to do your work. We live in an extension of the illusionary world in which you live. The outer rim of it. We are more in touch with the world of reality than you are. Spirit and mind belong to the world of reality. Everything else, that is, external things, are in a sense necessary for a time, but superfluous and only temporary as far as the world of reality goes. Spirit and mind belong to that world and are indestructible."

So there you have it. There are clearly many theories about what constitutes life in the next world. My own view falls on the side of the lucid dreamlike states. However, in essence the theories given by mediums, visionaries, philosophers, OBE travelers, and NDE cases all correspond in their basic ideas, though they may differ in the detail. The core of what I have tried to explain is that we experience a "state" in the afterlife that can also manifest as a "form."

I will now describe the "form" of some of the afterlife places you will visit. What follows is a composite of the ancient and modern visions put forward by mediums and seers. My "editor" for what follows is my own spirit guide Taratha, who has often guided this book during our trance sessions at my own circle. You will also now understand that your own experience of these afterlife places may differ slightly from what is described here, but the root experience will be intrinsically the same.

PLACES TO VISIT IN THE AFTERLIFE

"Roads go ever ever on, Over rock and under tree,
By caves where never sun has shone, By streams that never find
the sea;
Over snow by winter sown. And through the merry flowers of
June,
Over grass and over stone. And under mountains in the moon.
—J. R. R. TOLKIEN

REUNITING WITH FAMILY AND FRIENDS

Upon awakening from the cosmic sleep you will feel alive as ever. You will be met by your friends, family, and colleagues who made the transition before you. Naturally this will be a joyful experience. They will be dressed as you once knew them and at the age you remember them best. Your granddad, for example, may come as an old man, while a loved child will remain a child. Later you will discover that, in the afterlife world, we can live at any age we choose. Most probably prefer to exist in their prime; others may feel an affinity to a different age. Your bodily form easily shifts according to your will, as you are in reality a being of light. Recognizable forms, however, help in identifying each other and making family and friends feel more comfortable.

Naturally it will be a wonderful experience, meeting all of those people you have not seen for so long. The initial grief you may have experienced, at having to separate from loved ones left behind on earth, will be replaced by a feeling of great joy. The process of dying will seem far behind you, and you will marvel at the realization that everything you hold dear is within your grasp.

Meditation Exercise: Visualizing Your Entry into the Afterlife
For this experiment, you are going to visualize yourself meeting the people you love in the next life. Although this is an exercise in imagination rather than the development of mediumship, it will nonetheless help you get an idea of what the afterlife experience is like. Part of you has been to the afterlife before you came to the earth, so part of you already knows what the afterlife is like. That part is what you are trying to access with this exercise:

STEP 1. Read these instructions; then sit in a comfortable chair or lie down so that you can completely relax. As you close your eyes and breathe deeply, you feel yourself sinking deeper and deeper into a wonderful warm relaxation. All your troubles are gone, and you are now focused on the inner world.

STEP 2. With closed eyes, you use your inner vision to look all around you. You can see the landscape of a familiar beautiful place that you visited during your earthly life. Now it is even more beautiful than you remember. Look at the colors in the environment. See how they radiate such color and beauty. Everything exudes peace and contentment. Notice how comfortable the environment feels. You may see the sunshine lighting up the world around you. Notice how important light is in this place. Light here feels as if it is alive, as if it is the life force itself. You may hear birds and smell the fragrance of flowers.

STEP 3. You can feel yourself moving across this landscape. As you focus on a landmark, you feel yourself moving toward it. You move with grace and gentleness. Imagine how it would feel to have no troubles and worries. All the troubles of earthly life are gone. Tension, stress, ill health, and anxiety are impossible here. There is a feeling that everything is as it should be.

STEP 4. On the horizon, you see some figures. If you listen very carefully, you can hear them calling your name. You move a little closer to them and now hear their voices. The voices are familiar, of people you have loved. Drawing closer still, you begin to make out their faces. Your heart beats a little faster as you recognize the faces as those you love, who have come to this wonderful place before you. In enthusiasm, a pet breaks away from them and runs toward you, eager to be the first to greet you.

STEP 5. You are now very close to the group and can see their shining eyes and welcoming smiles. "It has been so long," you hear one of them say, in a familiar voice that you know so well. You notice that a simple low fence separates you from them. However, there is a gate. If you pass through this gate, you understand that there will be no going back to your old life. For a short moment, you think about the people on earth whom you would be leaving behind. You are aware that it is still possible for you to turn back, but you now have the reassuring innate knowledge that those you love will also one day pass through this gate. Once you pass through the gate, you will never be able to return.

STEP 6. (For now, however, with the full knowledge that this isn't actually our time, we will continue our practice journey.) You pass through the gate.

STEP 7. As you pass through the gate, notice the mixture of feelings you experience. There is anticipation, a sense of loss for those you leave behind, and a feeling of wonderful warm love as you embrace the people you love here in the afterlife.

Step 8. Finally, spend some time fantasizing about what you would say to the people you meet. What feelings would you express? What would you want to tell them? What do you think they would say to you about your life on earth; and what you could have accomplished to have made it better?

Step 9. Eventually, one of them looks at you with love and softly whispers, "It is time now to go back." Take with you the feelings and insights this visualization has given you. Some may come from your unconscious, but some may also come from the direct communication that occasionally happens when we are fully attuned. Now return to normal consciousness and make some written notes about any insights that you may have been given.

Step 10. Apply the insights to your life.

THE PLANE OF ILLUSION

You will discover that materials of this world are so pliable that they may be shaped by direct action of the imagination. If you wish something to be, it will form without needing a craftsman or designer. What you wish for will materialize.

Naturally, the things that materialize for you and the situations you find yourself in are based initially on your earthly experience. You will probably be drawn into situations that help you to resolve the inner conflicts and desires you had on earth. For example, Fredrick Myers, one of the founders of the Society of Psychical Research, was able to speak through a number of mediums after his death. In particular, he was able to prove the reality of the afterlife by giving messages to a number of mediums that only made sense when the messages were brought together. When the fragments were assembled, they easily fell into place, forming a clear communication, even though none of the mediums knew about each other or had any idea that there were other messages involved. This method became known as *cross-correspondence* and is solid proof of life after death.

In another communication, Myers tells us about a man named "Walter," who had been a wealthy stockbroker in his former life on earth. On awakening from the cosmic sleep, Walter continues to have the desire to make money, so he materializes a world around him similar to his earthly life. He meets his mother, who helps him to build an idealized version of his former life. Walter meets other souls who also loved the world of the stock market, and together they play the illusionary game of becoming multimillionaires.

On earth, being so rich brought admiration, but here in the heavenly planes, where money counts as nothing, Walter begins to realize his spiritual poverty. This produces in him a feeling of disappointed restlessness. Eventually, Walter realizes that, spiritually, he did not amount to much. He comes to understand that his suffering originated from his desires, which were partially brought on by his father's scorn and his mother's possessiveness. Becoming angry, he is desperate to escape. Walter is reborn on earth together with his mother, who in this incarnation is given the opportunity to redeem the damage her possessiveness had caused in the last.

Perhaps something similar will happen to you if you are motivated by powerful materialistic drives. During your cosmic sleep, you may have dreams and nightmares about your previous life. Worlds will be gestated while you are in this sleep state and become actualized when you awake. This transition from cosmic sleep to wakefulness Myers called the *journey down the long gallery.*

It is generated from your own memory and will include both good and bad states, depending on the memory content of your psyche.

When the incubation is complete, you will awaken to your customized version of the afterlife. Many of the things you will see will be familiar to you. For example, you may awaken to find yourself at home or in an environment in which you feel comfortable. The world around you will be just like the world you knew before. Later, this world will change as you become familiarized with your condition. However, a great many people continue with their old routines for a long period of time. For these people, the world of the afterlife is not very different from this world. They may continue to go shopping, eat food, and visit the bank or laundromat. If sex was important to you, then you may continue to make love with those of similar disposition. Even though your actual physical body is no more, you will generate a new one during this illusionary state of being.

You may want to linger in this plane of existence for a great deal of time. Some, I am sure, never progress beyond it, or may stay here for generations. Here you have the opportunity to resolve the things that you were unable to complete in life. You will meet others of like mind and perhaps develop new interests. You may develop a different family structure and take special interest in a religion, trade, science, or art. What is possible is only limited by your imagination.

Some may still appear to use language if they retain this attachment, but most people will communicate by telepathy. Because of this, you will easily befriend people who may have come from other countries in your former existence. As mentioned before, you will no longer be able to claim "My wife doesn't understand me" because you will be able to express yourself completely, and there will be no misunderstandings created by the limits of language.

It will be easy to recognize who is a good person and who is a bad one, as the soul will be transparent. Indeed, those with a beautiful disposition will be seen as the real "beautiful people." The beauty that may once have lain deep within is now revealed, clear for all to see. You will be judged by others by what you are, and no longer by what you "appear" to be.

SEX IN THE AFTERLIFE

As you can see, even on these first levels of the afterlife, there are many things that differ from our own world. As you begin to spiritually progress, you will gradually drop many of the trappings that you once knew. For example, you may decide that eating is a waste of time, as there is no body needing fuel. Those who enjoyed good food and drink in their earthly lives may continue to indulge for a while, but eventually they will see the foolishness of this activity. Without the impulses from the physical body, there is no hunger to satisfy.

Similarly, other bodily functions will fall by the wayside. What point is there in periodically going to the bathroom in the afterlife? At first, you may continue the routine as habit but, as you acclimate to your new world, you will eventually see it as completely unnecessary, too. For some people, sex may be a harder drive to let go of, since it involves psychological as well as physical drives. For many people, it may have been a very important part of their former lives, whereas others may have placed little importance upon it. In the final analysis, it is still a bodily function and may be let go of as your center of focus moves away from the physical illusion and toward the body of light.

You will discover that there are perhaps even more satisfying ways of expressing affection. Imagine the emotional satisfaction that might come with a complete telepathic blending of thought and feeling. It may sound a little like the sex scene from the movie *Sleeper* with Woody Allen, but spiritual "sex" is even more pleasurable as it involves the entire being. Furthermore, it is not a possessive act, as your interactions with everyone are based upon a transmission of love and energy.

Contemporary author Bruce Moen postulates some interesting ideas about sex in the afterlife. He pioneered a number of out-of-body travel techniques—based upon the methods of the Monroe Institute—that he claims put him in contact with the afterlife world and other nonphysical environments. During some of these journeys, he describes how he had spiritual sex with his companion, Sabrina. At first, their astral bonding was of the physical kind, which he knew on earth. However, it was suggested that they work with "sensing essence" and learn to blend their astral bodies completely. They experienced strange states such as leaping into flight as butterflies and mating in the form of dolphins. Eventually their light bodies intertwined as one. Moen describes it as an ecstatic experience: "We were spiraling around each other like strands of DNA. Immersed in feelings of loving acceptance as one being, we were enthralled with the dancing shades of pink, lavender, yellow, and blue swirling within us. All my internal resistance melted away in an indescribably powerful, heart-charging blast of Pure Unconditional Loving Acceptance as these two beings rejoined into One."

Unlike the accounts given by Spiritualists, Moen's accounts are hard to qualify as they are not generally substantiated by evidential mediumship and provable fact. Nonetheless, many of his ideas correlate with the nature of the afterlife as described by earlier traditions. The truth is that we can manipulate and change our form in the afterlife, which can result in many extraordinary and fantastic experiences.

The communications passed to me by our ex-physical loved ones is that the sex act is considered relatively unimportant in the afterlife. Men and women do have the same feelings for one another, but without the biological urge. Telepathy creates such a transparency of the soul that the most intimate expressions of love are given spontaneously and unconditionally. In effect, every act of communication is an act of love. In particular, the messages that are given to grieving partners on earth is that it's okay to get on with your life and take a new partner if that is what makes you happy. Love in the afterlife comes from the soul, and our earthly concerns about physical sex are of little import to those in the spirit. Often, spirit communicators who may have been possessive while on earth now advise the person they loved that he or she should seek a new partner. It is not the sex act that matters, but the love that goes with it. They tell us that, in the afterlife, we learn to love unconditionally and without covetousness or jealousy.

Each person will live in the afterlife dimensions in states that accord with his or her inner state of being. It is the place of the heart's desire; but the heart of man, as Kipling says, is small. Given that a person can create a world according to his own creativity, would it not be as limited as the individual himself?

At first, you may delight in the fact that all of your earthly wishes can come true. You may at last feel that you have found yourself; but there is an aftermath to this pleasurable state, for you will realize that these things are fundamentally selfish desires. The purpose of this phase of the afterlife journey is to bring an end to these personal emotions and desires so that you can move on to more permanent spiritual realizations. Eventually, the self-created enjoyments will lose their meaning and savor.

Nevertheless, when you first arrive in the heavenly planes, your desires will still hold you. For example, the routines of eating and drinking are too firmly established to be removed instantaneously. You may also feel the need to sleep. In the initial stages of the afterlife world, you may do all of these things. For some, the earthly pleasures may still be foremost in their consciousness, whereas others may want to quickly progress to "higher" spiritual states. A point may come when you have a longing to forsake this first plane of the afterlife and seek a greater reality. You will read about these states of being later, but first we will consider the planes of the afterlife that retain time, space, and form.

THE HALLS OF LEARNING

"And then it struck me that we are all children of Earth. It does not matter what country you look at. We are all Earth's children, and should treat her as our Mother."
—ALEKSANDR ALEKSANDROV (SOVIET COSMONAUT)

THERE IS A "STATE OF BEING" in the afterlife where you will have access to the accumulated knowledge of the ages. You will not only be able to look into the story of your own life and relive every experience, but you will also be able to see the complete narrative of the universe. Recorded in the vibrations of the cosmos is a record of everything that has happened.

Imagine what it would be like to see the rise and fall of the dinosaurs, or to witness the birth of civilization. How would you react to the carnage of the Roman Colosseum, the butchery of Genghis Khan, or the death camps of World War II? Imagine what it would be like to witness moments of great scientific breakthrough or feel the inspiration of the great artists. And, more important than the external history of civilization, how would you react to the inner evolution of humanity? You may ask yourself how much—or little—your life on earth contributed to a better world.

Now, as I have been at pains to point out, you will experience these stupendous things in a form that is easy for you to assimilate. You may experience it as a place. Some have called it the *great memory,* the *Akashic Record,* or the *spiritual libraries.* Mystics, mediums, and visionaries differ sometimes in the detail, but the following is based upon the general consensus. You may interpret this place according to your own understanding as the "mind stuff" molds to your own individual perceptions.

When you encounter the halls of learning, you will be astonished at the scale. At first you may see the place as a distant city on the horizon with its towers cutting into the strange incandescent skies of the afterlife. You may see stately buildings surrounded by magnificent gardens and trees. Some have spoken of the wonderful pools of glittering water that surround this place. You may look in wonder at them as they reflect every shade of every celestial color— some of which we have no names for here on earth.

As you move closer you will see that the streets are not bustling with life like the cities you have known. Instead, there is an unhurried atmosphere of contemplation and thoughtfulness. The buildings themselves are constructed according to the traditions of all the great cultures. There are the domes of Islam, the pillars of Greece and Rome, the stupas of India, the libraries of Alexandra, and the grandiose buildings of universities such as Oxford, Cambridge, Harvard, and Yale. You may also see modern structures and futuristic buildings. This place is a manifestation of the very essence of knowledge and learning.

THE DIVISIONS OF THE HALLS OF LEARNING

As with everything in the afterlife, the organization of this place is perfect. If you wish to know about a specific subject, you are drawn immediately to the source of the knowledge you need. You may suddenly find yourself inside one of the buildings and meeting one of the experts in the particular field you want to know about. A room will materialize around you, one perfectly suited to your disposition and the questions you want to ask. For example, if you want to know about alchemy, you may find yourself in an alchemist's laboratory from the Middle Ages. If literature is your chosen subject, you may meet your wise man or woman in a vast library of old books.

The halls of learning have many departments and sections that manifest according to the needs of each lecture or study. You will not think of this as a strange world, for the transition into these states will feel familiar and natural. Like educational establishments, the areas of the halls of learning have various sections and departments.

The Art Section

As a young man, I lived for some years as a painter and had a number of exhibitions around the United Kingdom. Unfortunately, circumstances made it impossible to complete the artistic career that once drove me so powerfully. I am sure that when my days on earth are done, one of the first things I will seek out in the next world is the afterlife haunts of artists.

Nestled among the halls of learning is a section that Spiritualists have called the *domain of artistic inspiration*. Made up of gleaming halls, here you will see the great masters at work as they are inspired by direct attunement with divine inspiration. The contemporary medium James Van Praagh describes this place succinctly: "It is here where these mediums of God's divine light synthesize and transform creative energy into materialized expressions of colors and words. These paintings are truly inspirational moments of color. One not only can view these works of art, but also completely feel all the love that flows from them."

The Science Section

Earthly science is the systematic study of the material world. Scientists encountering the paradoxical world of the afterlife plane inevitably have to make many adjustments to their conception of the world. For many with cherished materialistic beliefs, it may be difficult to accept that reality has this other facet. Shifting from an existence where the objective world is the reality to a state where the inner world takes precedent may be very difficult for some scientifically trained minds.

Nonetheless, the scientist who is truly in search of truth will see the afterlife world as a wonderful opportunity to continue his or her exploration of reality. According to many spirit guides, knowledge, like God, is infinite, so science cannot ever come to a final "all and everything" conclusion to the mystery of existence.

The scientific experiments that are undertaken in the afterlife are divorced from those that are conducted in the physical world because, at this level of being, people are concerned with the expression of the spirit rather than the study of matter. However, a scientist may apply the methodology he learned on earth to understanding the nature of the afterlife reality, as similar natural laws apply to both realities.

In the areas of the halls of learning dedicated to science, there is continuous experimentation to understand the nature of existence. And, just as we only have part of the truth in this world, in the spiritual realms there is still a great deal to discover and understand.

As the earth world is evolving, so too is the afterlife world.

The Literature Section

There are some people who have claimed that there is a special language in heaven. This idea was proposed during medieval times, and there is a somewhat dubious practice today of speaking in tongues. The Bible has references to these heavenly writings. For example, Ezekiel (II: 9, 10) says: "When I looked, behold a hand put forth by a spirit to me; and in it the roll of a book which he unfolded in my sight; and it was written on the front and on the back."

According to the Swedish philosopher Swedenborg, writing in the 1740s, the words are written in a special language that appears upon the page as the writer thinks them. (I would certainly find this handy.) Swedenborg says: "A little paper was once sent to me from heaven, on which were written only a few words in Hebrew characters, and it was said that every letter involved arcana of wisdom; and that those arcana were contained in the inflections and curvatures of the letters, and thus also in the sounds."

Swedenborg considered this to be divine language. He also claimed that this language was known to the ancients before the invention of writing as we know it. It is an angelic language. Its vowels express affections and its consonants reflect ideas. These writings are permanent, whereas there is also a language that is used for day-to-day communication that dissolves once it has served its purpose. Swedenborg claimed also that there is a language of heaven that consists of nothing but numbers; a spiritual sense that consists of a spiritual significance number and then a series of numbers. Swedenborg may have been thinking of numerology, yet unexpectedly anticipating computer language. He certainly believed that the inventions made on earth were predated by their spiritual counterparts in the heavenly worlds.

I would like to think that language is still appreciated in the afterlife. After all, we need some way to store ideas and present new ones. My personal view is that the heavenly language is a reflection of ideas that are forever present in the afterlife. They are a manifested form of thought. Some may perceive this as language and enjoy the familiar functions of writing and reading. A "book" in the spirit is the essence of an idea that can be "read" by anyone in whatever language or form that appeals most. Perhaps you would prefer to experience this cosmic knowledge as a television program, an IMAX movie, or even made into a comic book!

The Music Section

The famous Spiritualist medium and healer Harry Edwards explains how he was once shown where a musical concert was being conducted near the halls of learning. Again, this seemed a strange world consisting of a mixture of thought and form. He attempts to describe the somewhat surreal musical instrument that will transmit the concert:

"John then noticed the strange structure. It was taller than a man, and as wide in width. The nearest thing which John could liken it to was a tower with a broad base and narrowing towards the top where two arm-like tentacles emerged from the sides. At the end of the tentacles was a silvery mass of slender stamen-like stalks, which in turn had scores upon scores of very fine gossamer-like hairs. John thought to himself they looked like overgrown dandelion blooms waiting for someone to come along and 'blow' on them."

Later we are told that this tower-like structure is a vehicle for receiving the musician's thoughts, which are telepathically transmitted as music. The music is the spontaneous creation of the master musician's mind and the other orchestral telepaths. The music in this spiritual amphitheater is beautiful beyond compare because it is experienced directly. It is a heartfelt expression of the divine. You experience the "music" as a pure blending of your awareness with that of the musician.

THESE STRANGE WORLDS

Much of our earlier discussions have been based mainly on accounts from Spiritualist literature. However, a person from the twenty-first century may not see "books" at all but experience the halls of learning as a vast computer complex, or some form of spiritual Internet. And why should the halls be placed in an earth-like setting? The great temple could just as easily be a glass dome on a vast spaceport at the center of the universe or in a nebula, floating over a cosmic sea, or perhaps isolated in the blackness of intergalactic space. Here you will have access to computers that will provide you with all the knowledge you can handle.

Spiritualist ideas about a place we go to learn appear to be substantiated by the reports of subjects who have had near-death experiences. For example, one of Dr. Raymond Moody's subjects described how "it was like I knew all things . . . I thought whatever I wanted to know could be known." Another subject described "libraries" and "institutions of higher learning": "This is the place where the PLACE is knowledge . . . It's like you focus mentally on one place in that school and—zoom—knowledge flows by you from that place automatically. It's just like you'd had about a dozen speed-reading courses."

The world described above is, in many ways, similar to the material world we know. The philosopher Rudolf Steiner condemned this way of thinking saying that "the Spiritualists are the greatest materialists of all!" However, we should continually remind ourselves of the problem of trying to translate new perceptions into words. The spirit people and the NDE subjects are describing a state of being that is hard to express in words. Our understanding of the earthly world is closely bound up with language, whereas most reports agree that language in the afterlife is unnecessary. Is it any wonder then that we are, in a way, seeing "through a glass darkly."

HOW YOU WILL PERCEIVE THE AFTERLIFE

"Then one is struck with a marvelous light, one is received into pure regions and meadows."

—PLUTARCH

ONE OF THE THINGS THAT NDE researchers have found is that fear is not the dominant emotion in most dying patients. There is sometimes discomfort and pain, but a surprisingly large number are elated at the time of death, even to the point of rapture and seeing visions. According to Dr. Karlis Orsis, these reports of a final euphoria amount to about one in twenty deaths. Most of these patients, fully awake, described visions of the next life. They saw beautiful landscapes, heard birds singing, and often expressed sentiments such as "I want to go back."

Reports given us by NDE subjects and ancient and modern seers tell us that the world of the afterlife is like our own world but that certain things we take for granted are fundamentally different. What follows now is a composite of these ideas, to give you an overview of the world you will experience. I have touched upon some of these subjects in other places throughout the book, but here is a simple summary, together with some additional information.

LIGHT

Compared to the light of heaven, the sun of our world appears dark. In our reality, our sun produces light by nuclear reaction. Our sun's spiritual equivalent in the afterlife is the light of love. According to Swedenborg, what the spirit people perceive as the sun is in fact the light of God. There, the sun is the radiance of love, whereas the moon is the radiance of faith.

Some mediums say that there is no sun in the spirit world. There is eternal day, as everything radiates its own light so that there is no need of a sun. It is an incandescent world. Sometimes the light darkens for a time so that those who still need to sleep may do so. In the higher realms of the afterlife all is light, so there is no distinction between light and dark, day or night. In the nether regions darkness prevails, and the light of the higher planes is intolerable to those who shun the light of love.

The main thrust of creation is not physical evolution but spiritual evolution. Those who have cast off all association with physical form will move into an abundant, energetic life with no physical form at all. This will be a state of being that is best described as a world of pure light. However, the word "light" can only partly express the brilliance of the luminescence of the beyond, for it is not a natural light as we know it; it is pure spiritual light. The brilliance of the light you will see varies according to your receptivity to divine truth, for the light radiates not from a sun but from the creator.

COLOR

The communications made by Fredrick Myers to the Society of Psychical Research reveal some interesting things about color in the afterlife. He says: "A human being cannot imagine a new sound, or a new color, or a feeling entirely outside the range of his previous experience. It is impossible for him to conceive the infinite variety of new sounds, colors, and feelings experienced by us." In addition, Myers talks about a whole realm of existence that he calls the *fourth plane* or the *Eidos*—a plane of color.

The afterlife worlds are filled with exquisite colors that are not seen on earth and become more incredible as you ascend to the higher levels. Everything is more intense and highly energized. A person who progresses to the "plane of color" no longer needs to sleep, and the environment expresses love, truth, and beauty. The main work on the "plane of color" is toward understanding how the mind controls energy and the life force from which the outward manifestation of the afterlife world is created.

Spirit communicators have told me that the form and color of the spirit world are somewhat similar to those in our world, but what is indescribable is the feelings they evoke. Have you ever had a time in your life when you suddenly got an overwhelming feeling that you could only describe as a sense of joy and uplift? It would not last long, but it is just a taste of the feelings that you will have all the time in the afterlife planes.

SOUND AND LANGUAGE

Sound has a much richer nature than the sounds we experience on earth. There are frequencies of sound that we could not even begin to imagine. It is hard for us to comprehend the beauty of the music that is played in the afterlife, as mentioned earlier when I spoke of the halls of learning. Similarly, in the higher planes of the afterlife, music permeates the worlds of light. Here we experience the delights of the angels "singing." In reality, it is a musical expression of the blissful thoughts of those who know the infinity of God. In the East, they claim that the sound that most expresses the highest state of spirituality is the mantra "Om." It is similar to the Christian word "Amen" and reverberates in the background, expressing the totality of all things.

One of the main uses of sound during earthly life is of course language. In the afterlife, language becomes obsolete. The way communication works in the afterlife is expressed in an interesting communication from the spirit of Fredrick Myers who says: "I have but to concentrate my thought for what you might call a moment and I can build up a likeness of myself, send that likeness speeding across our vast world to a friend, to one, that is, in tune with me. Instantly I appear before that friend, though I am remote from him. My likeness holds speech—in thought, remember, not words—with this friend. Yet, all the time, I control it from an enormous distance; and as soon as the interview is concluded I withdraw the life of my thought from that image of myself, and it vanishes."

HEAT AND COLD

According to Swedenborg, the heat of the afterlife is like the light described earlier, in that it is everywhere varied and different according to your receptivity to divine truth. It differs in each level of the afterlife in both degree and quality. The heat in the heavenly realms is the fire of divine love. In the "hell" planes it manifests as the fire of hatred. Coolness corresponds with divine peace, but the absence of heat corresponds to being separated from divine love.

The Spiritualist thinker Arthur Findlay, who sat with the direct-voice medium John Sloan, postulated a similar idea, saying that there are eight different suns in Etheria (the afterlife). One of these is our own sun, which is "a rotating globe surrounded by, and interpenetrated by, seven other rotating globes. . . . Each surface in Etheria receives the light from the etheric sun's surface to which it is attuned."

Findlay is talking about different lights in different levels of the afterlife. Again, I believe we are here in a situation where words and images are not adequate to describe sensations outside our usual experience. Others have described the heat of heaven differently. I suppose the warmth we feel in this heavenly world is akin to simile used in describing the warmth of the human heart. I am reminded of the classic story from India of blind men trying to describe an elephant. One wraps his arms around the elephant's leg and exclaims that the elephant is like a tree. Another, touching the elephant's side, insists that it's like a wall. And a third, holding the trunk, exclaims that it is like a rope.

We are in a similar quandary when we try to describe experiences that are beyond the reach of our normal senses.

TIME

From the standpoint of consciousness, the past is just a memory and the future is an expectation. The only reality we can be certain about is that there is "now." I believe that this awareness of the "now" still continues in the afterlife worlds. However, in the higher levels of the afterlife, all events happen simultaneously. There is a timeless state in which past, present, and future become one. There may also be states of being that are beyond time and space and therefore impossible for us, with our reasoning, to comprehend.

Although all things in the afterlife have their successions and progressions as in this world, the advanced spirits move beyond time and space. According to some sources, the angels do not even know what time and space are. For beings who have progressed to this level, there are not days and years, only changes of state of being. Eternity is not an infinite time, it is an infinite state.

The messages we have received from mediumship indicate that the spirit people are aware of linear time. For those on the first planes of the afterlife, time still moves from the past through the present and into the future. However, the sense of the passing of time is different. For example, loved ones who have passed to the spirit world reassure us that they feel no suffering when they consider the wait that comes before they can be reunited with their loved ones on earth. For them the time from the moment they died to the time we join them feels like only an instant.

It would appear that time in the spirit is relative to the state of consciousness being experienced. It is perhaps an extended perception of time as we know it on earth. When Einstein was asked to explain relativity to the layman, he may have inadvertently also described the way time is experienced in the next life: "Put your hand on a hot stove for a minute and it seems like an hour. Sit with a pretty girl for an hour and it seems like a minute. That's relativity."

The spirit people tell us that they cannot predict the future. It is in our own hands. They may, however, recognize the trends happening in our lives and give advice about the best course to follow; but they cannot make predictions. Spiritualism is clear about this. Each individual has to take "personal responsibility" for his or her life—a principle that includes free will. Part of the training of mediums is to urge them not to use fortune-telling as part of their mediumship demonstrations. (Even with my extensive background and experience, although I often do predictions work for my own sitters, I never mix mediumship with what I call "psychic counseling.")

I have spoken earlier about the record of the past that some call the *Akashic Record*. This is a theosophical concept, which refers to the spiritual record of all worldly events and personal experiences. (*Akasha* is taken from a Sanskrit word meaning "luminous.") It is conceived of as an omnipresent medium—similar to the ether of nineteenth-century physics—that acts as a cosmic memory. Attunement with the Akashic record will enable you to be aware of your own personal history and of the history of everything that has ever happened.

SPACE

People often ask me, "How big is the afterlife?" It can be answered by asking a similar question: "How big is a dream?" "A dream has no size," you say. So it is with the afterlife. Like a dream, the afterlife world is a "state" of being, so it can be as big or as small as you want it to be. The form of the afterlife is created by consciousness. Our minds have complete control of our surroundings. As we think, so we become. I also believe that this is the material destiny of man and that one day we will have complete mental control of time and space in this world we live in now.

In the higher spiritual planes, the angelic inhabitants have evolved beyond place and space. They may appear to move normally, but it is in effect their state that changes. The societies in each level of heaven are aware of this reality to different degrees. In some planes, reality is very similar to the world we are experiencing now. All things appear in place and in space exactly as they do in the world. However, for some people, the afterlife is a fluid place that is molded and changed by consciousness. The highest states of all are completely formless.

CLOTHES

I recall giving a consultation to a lady whose dead husband showed himself in full Masonic regalia. This was important proof to the woman, as her husband had a keen interest in Freemasonry and had been a member of the Grand Lodge in London. Interestingly, the spirit person went on to say that he still attends his Lodge meetings in the afterlife. He explained that the "secrets" were not secrets at all but were states of being that could only be understood by people who were able to realize them. To the rational mind, these states "appeared" to be secrets. The objective of afterlife Freemasonry, he said, was to unite individuals with the "greatest secret" by making them aware of the grand architect of the universe, whom some call God.

People can dress as they like in the afterlife. White robes are not the obligatory uniform. Just as we manifest in the afterlife according to our thoughts, so too clothes appear from the imagination. You are most likely to wear the type of clothing that you used to wear during your life. Nonetheless, I would imagine that some people, for whom clothes were important, will manifest clothing according to their personal tastes. And without regard now to either cost or availability, the afterlife may be full of elaborate costumes. Who knows what designers and fashions there are in the next world?

The spirit communicators who have made themselves known through my mediumship have always shown themselves in the earthly clothes they once wore, so this is the limitation of my knowledge. However, some mediums and Spiritualist thinkers have spoken of heavenly clothes that are worn by the higher beings and angels. The angels are said to wear clothing that is symbolic of a higher state of spiritual perfection. The garments they choose to wear to clothe themselves also come from their advanced intelligence; therefore they are even more beautifully clad. Their clothing is said to shine with white light, because white corresponds to goodness. The angels of the inmost heaven are not clothed, because they exist in total innocence, which corresponds to the complete openness of nudity.

In the lower, hell-like planes, clothes reflect the lower consciousness of the people from these planes. They appear in garments that are ragged, squalid, and filthy.

MONEY

In a world where the mind can create whatever you may want, there is clearly no need for money. However, some people may still have such an attachment to money that they will continue to use it. The desire for money can restrict a person's spiritual progress and make it hard for them to ascend to the higher spiritual states (such as the man named "Walter" mentioned earlier, related from the spirit of Fredrick Myers, who continued to work the stock market even in the afterlife).

Some may continue to use money, just as some will continue to eat or go to the toilet. These souls are still trapped in their illusionary worldly attachments.

FAME

My own work as a medium brings me into contact with all sorts of people from all walks of life. Most of the time I have no idea with whom I am dealing. Many of my consultations are done from my home, over the Internet, or when I go to visit people in their own homes. Occasionally, I will visit London to do consultations for people if they can assemble a group of four. Soon after the death of Princess Diana, a lady from Knightsbridge in London rang me for a "party plan" group of consultations. The private consultations would be done at her office. (I will call her Sylvia.)

When it came time for Sylvia to have her "reading," she told me that she would like me to try to get in touch with her mother on the spirit side. I gave the reading knowing nothing about Sylvia's background or life. I made a communication with her mother and gave some proof that she could accept. However, I had to interrupt our reading because someone else was trying hard to get through. I had to put her in touch with a young lady who had just passed to the spirit world in a terrible car accident. As I continued to describe the woman and the details about her passing, I realized it was the spirit of Princess Diana that was communicating with us.

At the time, I had no idea that Sylvia was a close friend of Diana's and had been one of her health advisors—using New Age techniques. When the press had originally heard about Diana's involvement in this, they staked out the building in the hope of exposing the story of Diana's interest in what they perceived to be weird ideas.

I described Diana to Sylvia, but I needed some unique evidence to prove her identity.

I felt a little embarrassed about the idea, as so many mediums claim to be in contact with celebrities, without providing supporting evidence as proof that it is the actual spirit who is speaking and not a figment of the medium's imagination. I gave Sylvia the following pieces of evidence to prove with whom I was in contact:

1. I quoted lines from a letter that I said Elton John had written—a copy of which was now in Sylvia's possession.

2. Similarly, I quoted from a letter from Barbara Cartland.

3. I gave Sylvia the typical greeting that Diana would say to her.

4. I told her how they had discovered that they had been bugged. According to Sylvia, the British Secret Service had been carefully monitoring all of Diana's movements and conversations long before she met Dodie Al Fayed. Diana believed that this was not merely for her personal protection but that there was a hidden agenda to keep a lid on her rebellious spirit.

5. I repeated sentences from the conversation Sylvia and Diana had in which the princess had confessed that, despite it all, she still loved Charles—a fact that she had confessed to Sylvia when they were alone.

6. I said that Diana took pleasure in taking trinkets from the palace and giving them to her friends. In particular, I said that she had given Sylvia two small silver-and-gold pillboxes. They had royal initials on the bottom and had once belonged to Russia's Romanov family. I described the lids of the boxes, likening the decorations to a blue cameo.

When the sitting was over, Sylvia went to another room and returned with some envelopes of materials. From them, she selected and showed me photocopies of the letters and the words I had quoted. In addition, she pulled out a color photograph. It was of the two small Romanov pillboxes that Sylvia had been given by Diana. The inscriptions and everything I had said about them were correct.

I was, of course, flabbergasted that Diana had come through during this run-of-the-mill consultation. At a time so close to her passing, and while the nation still mourned, it seemed almost in bad taste. The nation had already had enough of psychics revealing Diana's most intimate secrets.

There is usually a reason for a spirit to make a communication. The most important is to let the grieving know that they are safe in the new life and that the tragedy that struck them is no longer causing them pain. Unfortunately, I was unable to communicate with Dodie, although Diana wanted people to know that they were both safe in the new life. She passed to me a message, which I conveyed to Sylvia, saying: "Dodie and I were deeply in love. But our love could never have flowered as it should have done in the world. Only here, in the bliss of the afterlife, can our love find its fulfillment." I also gave Sylvia a few personal messages via Diana for Dodie's father. I hope that somehow they were received.

Diana's spirit struck me as completely different from what I would have imagined. Rather shocked, I said to Sylvia that Diana had a tendency to swear a great deal and would delight in using bad language. Sylvia told me that, away from the limelight, Diana was quite a colorful character and indeed did swear a lot when they came together. In the comfort of Sylvia's consultation room, she relaxed and could let off steam as much as she liked.

Diana said how she loved her boys, but I was surprised when she said she loved Charles. She was of course "in love" with Dodie, but she wanted it to be known that she had never hated or not loved Charles. He was a man she wanted to love, but from the start Camilla Parker-Bowles, his mistress, had stood in the way.

Finally we asked her about the claims that there had been a conspiracy to kill her. Having heard that MI5 had once bugged Sylvia's rooms, I was expecting dark tales of intrigue. Diana was emphatic in saying that, as far as she was aware, there was no conspiracy to kill her.

What happened was a tragic accident, but it is good to be aware that Diana and Dodie are safe and well in the afterlife. I hope that Al Fayed and others who grieve for the couple may one day come to understand that there was no place for them in this world but that there was a place for them in the next. The power of love found a way for them to be together, but it was not for us to share. The contemporary medium Patricia Kirmond expressed it well when she said, about Diana's death, "Sometimes what appears to human consciousness to be a tragedy is, in the divine sense, the fulfilling of the karmic equation for that particular soul."

So what did Diana's spirit have to say about what happens to famous people when they die? I wondered about the fact that so many people were thinking about her and grieving for her. Did she feel all this grief? How could she stand it? I repeated to Sylvia what I heard Diana saying: "Here we are protected from the thoughts of all the people who are grieving for us. We could never stand it. I am now just like anyone else. I am not a princess or an ex-wife or a "scheming actress," I am who I am—the real me. Here, fame makes absolutely no difference. Already I understand this. What matters is who I am and what I feel. At the moment all I am concerned about—apart from the boys—is that I can be with the person I love. And nobody can stop us being together."

HEAVENLY SOCIETY

As the above example illustrates, fame means nothing in the afterlife. Simply because you have been a royal person or a president or a great leader does not mean that you will carry this status into the next life. Your true worth is based upon who you have become. In the afterlife, falsehood fails, truth triumphs, and virtue reigns. Character confers power—not knowledge, inventive skill, or wealth. The next world is guided by wisdom.

The afterlife world is an organized place with its own social structures and even a government. However, it is unlike any administration known on earth.

Social Order

Imagine the potentially chaotic situation at the initial stages of the afterlife. A continual stream of new arrivals includes the wise, the wicked, the learned, and the insane. Many are likely to be puzzled or in a state of confusion. Fortunately, the spirit world has been around for a long time and is well organized, with knowledgeable leadership.

The life review has already revealed that, from the moment you pass over, you will have a chaperone to the next life. At your entry to the next world, you meet your guardian angel and are made aware of your life on earth and what to expect during your stay in the afterlife planes. What you encounter at that initial orientation is just a small part of the hierarchy of spiritual organization that you will discover exists as you move through the afterlife realities.

In earthly life, it is power and money that usually confers position in society. We honor people with wealth, social class, business acumen, and talent. Yet many of these individuals are not worthy of our tribute. Political cunning, ruthless business tactics, and clever manipulation of others have been known to cause a person to rise to a position of recognition and respect in our world. In the afterlife, these ambitious attitudes are considered to be bad qualities, and do not in any way improve your status in the next world.

Some individuals may continue to have fantasies about power and create illusionary worlds in which they appear to be living out their ambitions. These illusionary states, however, will contain fundamental flaws that enable the higher spirit beings to make the soul-dreamer aware of the futility of his desire. The influential New Age pioneer Gary Zukav put it succinctly when he wrote: "The illusion is exquisitely intimate to the needs of each soul. Always each situation serves each person involved. You cannot, and will not, encounter a circumstance, or a single moment, that does not serve directly and immediately the need of your soul to heal, to come into wholeness."

Some, in order to avoid confronting their misconceptions, may reincarnate immediately, returning to earthly suffering and missing out on the blissful afterlife states.

People with similar motivations will be drawn together and create between them, through their own megalomaniac desires, their own worlds. The snag is that everyone wants to rule, resulting in continual conflict, competition, and hatred. They may think all is well—as it should be—but if they can examine their hearts, they will see that they are suffering. The worst thing about being in hell is not knowing that you are there in the first place, and that you are creating the illusion yourself.

In the spiritual planes, it is not our ability to rule but our ability to serve that counts. Returning to the case of Princess Diana, she had a high position in British society by right of her birth and marriage. Nonetheless, in her life she demonstrated compassion for others and influenced a great many people around the world to adopt better principles. She had many faults, but I'm sure her standing in the afterlife will be one of honor and respect. The personal touches she gave AIDS victims, and the comforting words and care she offered to children in distress will be, in retrospect, of far greater importance than all the high-ranking engagements and public events she ever attended. In the afterlife, we rise to status according to the qualities of our character.

Government

The spirit guides and helpers who have spoken through countless mediums all speak of the "natural law" that dictates the conditions in the next world. This natural law creates the right conditions spontaneously. For example, thoughts of anger will weigh heavy on some people and pull them into a pit of their own hatred until they are able to resolve these things. Similarly, thoughts of love will draw them upward to the higher levels of the spiritual kingdom. The natural law also draws people together who have similar motivations and dispositions. And it is the natural law that decides who, in the afterlife, will have eminence.

Those of good character and who are willing to serve will naturally attain position. This is not a democratic society where every person gets to vote—and where deception is possible. Here, all stand revealed and so take their rightful places in the hierarchy of the afterlife naturally—in a way impossible in the material world. Through the workings of this natural law, not unlike oils of differing purities separating in a glass container, the good automatically rise to position, while the bad sink to what is suitable for them. Those with a negative disposition cannot rise to the higher levels of the spirit to interfere with the organization of the higher planes. They are weighted down by their negativity. Advanced beings, however, if it is their wish, may descend to help those in the lower planes progress upward toward greater spirituality.

The beings that administer justice in the afterlife are those who have attained divine realization. Their hearts are at one with their conscience. It is character that gives power and love that is the touchstone of the law. The hierarchy of the heavenly government is dictated according to greatness of soul. Those who are closer to spiritual perfection naturally rise to the top of the political structure; yet their desire is not to rule but to serve.

PET HEAVEN

"All life is one. The divine spirit animates all who share this planet and we have responsibilities towards each other. You cannot divide life into watertight, right compartments. All aspects of life, man and animal, must move forward together. The animal cannot be left behind while man makes his evolutionary ascent."
—SILVER BIRCH (THE AMERICAN INDIAN GUIDE OF JOURNALIST MAURICE BARBANELL)

150

SOMETIMES, AT NIGHT, MY WIFE Jane sees the spirit of our dog William lying by the side of our bed. He still comes back and visits her. I also have received hundreds of letters and e-mails from people asking if their pets have survived death, and from people who believe that they have seen their dead pet's spirit.

In my mediumistic work, I have frequently had cause to describe and name animals during public demonstrations or private sittings. Pets are often shown to me in order to add that little extra bit of evidence to the identity of the human spirit communicator. I have seen many people cry when they realize that their cherished pet is not lost forever, but will be there for them when they return to the spirit world.

It is my opinion that pets do survive death and continue to live with us in the spirit world. Let me illustrate this with an example that was quoted in a national British magazine after being confirmed by a journalist. I have changed the name to protect the woman's identity:

"Traveling such a long way to see the medium Craig Hamilton-Parker felt a little odd. Particularly as I wanted to communicate with my little ten-year-old fox terrier dog, Pip, who died two years ago," says Susan Lloyd.

"I had no sense of Pip's spirit when he died, which came as a shock. I'd always assumed his spirit would be around in some way that I'd be able to feel. So I worried that he was lost somewhere, looking for me but unable to reach me. For a long time I was very upset.

"I had also recently lost my good friend Dave. I sat with him as he died and he talked frankly with me about the next life. He also loved terriers, and I told him how he would soon meet the dogs he'd lost in the afterlife.

"Dave's death was the catalyst. I worried that I may have been wrong about the spirit dogs. I needed to know whether the things I'd said to Dave were true.

"I said nothing to the medium about anything on my mind, but Craig told me all about Dave, his personality, the way he died, and how he had left a wife and three children.

"However, his main communicator was my friend Carol. Craig put his hands on his chest and said, 'Carol is telling me that at the time of her passing everything was falling apart. She gives me the feeling of suffocation. She was severely depressed and regrets to say that she took her own life.' I was amazed. Carol, who had been one of my oldest friends, had committed suicide five years previously and had confided in me about the black moods that haunted her.

"As Craig made the link, he took on Carol's mannerisms and posture. His voice and particularly his laugh sounded just like hers. Eventually, Craig said that Carol had an important message for me. 'Carol says that she wants to bring forward your dog. He is white and has a distinctive black patch on his tail. I can't hear his name but it has only three letters. She says it looks like the dog in a cartoon. Tin Tin perhaps?'

"This was the proof I was waiting for. I was a little worried because Carol didn't like animals when she was alive. But Craig put my mind at rest: 'Carol is happy because she is now safe. She wants you to know that your dog does not belong to her or to Dave. She brought him through because she knows how much you love him and vice versa. You have nothing to worry about concerning Pip.'

"I was able to drive back home with my mind at rest. I finally knew that Dave and Pip were safe and that Carol had at last found peace."

WHERE DO THE ANIMALS GO?

Before the Chinese occupation of Tibet, the people there used to sieve the soil when building temples so that not a single worm would be harmed. The Tibetans believed that souls can reincarnate in any living form, and that a human birth is a very rare and fortunate opportunity. In fact, the number of births a soul takes is so immense that one of the worms may have once been your mother in a past life.

A modern Tibetan Buddhist would probably say that it is unlikely that your mother will reincarnate as a worm, but will tell you that the Tibetans' actions are symbolic, to illustrate how we should have compassion for all sentient beings—as if they were our beloved kin. It also poses the question whether our soul climbs up an evolutionary ladder across many species. On one occasion, someone asked my spirit guide during a trance session what happened to the souls of all the dinosaurs. The guide's reply was, "They are as here now!" The point being that the human soul is, in fact, a later stage of an evolutionary process that has been going on since life began.

Some of the ancient Greek philosophers believed in *metempsychosis*: the slow evolution of the soul from animal to human form after many lower-species incarnations. It is a belief in many Eastern religions, and my mediumistic communications appear to agree with this. However, I question at what point a living thing becomes self-aware and capable of sustaining this awareness after death. For example, does a flea have a spirit?

My spirit guide has told us that animals do not all survive as individual identities after death. Some merge to what he calls a *group consciousness*. Their spirits return to a collective awareness for that particular species, and from this pool of awareness different animal souls are born. It is only when an animal becomes self-aware that its soul continues after death and starts the long process of climbing the evolutionary ladder toward human and angelic consciousness.

For many animals, this journey begins if it receives love from a human. In particular, pets and domestic animals gain a sense of identity because of prolonged exposure to humans. Our consciousness "rubs off" on them, so to speak, causing them to forsake much of their instinctive nature and start to develop free will. Some people lavish love on their pets and treat them like their own children. Although in many ways this is a form of psychological transference, they are in fact helping the animal progress spiritually. The love they lavish on them enables the pet to quickly attain a sense of identity. The owner is thereby helping to create a new soul. I suppose you could say that pets are children in a real sense, for their souls are brand new!

CHILDREN'S HEAVEN

One, two, three, four, five, six, seven,
All good children go to heaven.

—T<small>RADITIONAL NURSERY RHYME</small>

W<small>HEN LIFE HAS SERVED ITS</small> purpose, death must come. None of us can escape this fact. Even the holy men, saints, and saviors must die. When death comes it shows that the individual is ready to enjoy all the wonderful riches and beauty that the spirit world has to offer. There is nothing to fear in death. Death is the great liberator that brings freedom. We rejoice when babies come into the world, yet many cry in the world of spirit when babies are to be born in our world. Similarly, there may be weeping when someone dies in our world, but there is rejoicing as the spirit enters the sphere of the afterlife.

Losing someone you love is always a terrible thing. No matter how philosophical we are about it and no matter how much we are convinced that there is an afterlife, it is always a dreadful blow. But the hardest loss to bear of all is surely the loss of a child. There is often a lump in my throat and sometimes tears in my eyes when I do mediumship for bereaved parents. Mediumship in these circumstances can also be quite difficult because the child in the spirit does not have the concentration or understanding to work with a medium. There are occasions when it is impossible to make the link despite my best efforts and the goodwill of the sitter. Until the grief has been healed, it is very hard sometimes to give the mother her sought-after link with her child.

Fortunately, on most occasions the spirit child is able to communicate despite the walls of grief and despair built around

154

the parents. This is usually because more experienced spirit communicators are helping them. Sometimes it is the spirit guides who do the work, but on most occasions I have noticed that a deceased relative is aiding them.

This does not mean to say that all their time in the spirit world is spent with, for example, a deceased grandmother. The communicating spirit lets us know that he or she is with the child, but the child will also experience a wonderful world especially designed for children. The medium Doris Stokes, who herself lost a baby, often spoke of these children as the lucky ones. Unlike us, they do not have to suffer the problems of life. They come to us for a short while, experience our love, then return again to a better place. These children are well-developed souls who need only a short contact with the earth in order for them to spiritually progress. As Doris often said, "They are souls that kiss the earth."

In the afterlife, children naturally share the love of their grandparents and other spirit people who love them. They also have the guiding hand of their guardian angel to guide them. However, there are many activities for them in the next life designed to quicken their spirit and guide them toward higher spirituality.

I spoke earlier about how we can assume any age that we want to when we are in the spirit. Many of the souls of children have also lived many lives before, and they, like us, will have a long history of life behind them. However, they continue their heavenly life in the same form as they had on earth. They remain as children and grow in the spirit. Naturally, this state will not last indefinitely, but these souls need to experience innocence while in the ethereal states. The life review is unnecessary for many of these children. A short earthly life is the catalyst for a childhood in the spirit.

When children show the spirit via mediumship, they appear to the medium as they were when they died. This helps the parents to recognize the medium's description of their son or daughter. Once this is established, a child will sometimes then allow a description of the person they have grown into. The parents will also recognize that this description is often as they would have expected. For example, the spirit "adult" will explain that he or she spends the time involved with music. The adults may have noticed, before the child died, a natural tendency toward this field of study. It rarely surprises parents when told what their child is like now.

Babies grow in the afterlife. According to many spirit guides, and including my own, the soul enters a mother's womb not at the moment of conception but at the time of the "quickening"—the increasing movement of the coming child. It is often my difficult duty to explain that the soul who incarnated in a later aborted child continues to live in the next life. Rarely is there any finger-wagging or chastisement by the spirit communicator for what has been done. The child, who by this time has grown or has been brought forward by an adult spirit communicator, understands the circumstances that resulted in the termination. In most instances, an abortion is not something a woman enters into lightly. It is a tremendously anguished decision to be made, and some women carry a burden of guilt throughout their lives. The spirit people understand these painful feelings and do not stand in judgment. Instead, they reassure us that the soul of the baby continues and that the mother need not feel guilt. If there is an instinctive sense of love, then the soul of the parents and the child will be linked. Often parents may feel the soul of the child around them during earthly life. And they will certainly know the child when they enter the spirit world themselves.

There are many places in the afterlife that children will enjoy. We are told that there are nurseries where the spirit people, who devote their time to the care of the young, tend the babies. Here walk many angels who help with the development of these innocent souls. There is great love in this place, and the children are made aware of their earthly mother and family and are able to share their thoughts and feelings. Indeed, they are bound to the family's group soul by karma and past life experiences together. (This will be explained in more detail later.)

Education in the afterlife is spiritual rather than practical. Children are taught the importance of the development of the spirit and are taught human values. This is an important part of the soul's progress that can only be experienced while living the life of a child in the spirit. The primal form, which I spoke about earlier, is temporarily suspended so that the soul can learn the lessons that can only be understood while in a state of innocence. This takes place in areas of the halls of learning that are designated for the spiritual development of children.

ANGELS AND DEVILS

"With hideous ruin and combustion, down
To bottomless perdition, there to dwell."
—JOHN MILTON (*Paradise Lost*)

HELL, AND WHAT TO DO IN THE LOWER PLANES

Tell people that they will go to hell if they do not convert to your particular brand of religion and you'll soon have converts knocking at your door. Sadly, many religions have used the fear of retribution to threaten their flocks. The New Age philosopher David Ike summed it up for me when we met on a television show called *Mystic Challenge*: "Religion is the most sophisticated form of brainwashing ever invented."

Perhaps the hellfire preachers are right, and I will perish in some terrible pit in hell. Perhaps I should donate large sums of money to their causes to save me from my Faustian fate. Nonetheless, if I am to go to the sulphurous pit, I'm likely to meet some interesting people in this netherworld, including perhaps Homer, Socrates, Gandhi, Mohammed, Einstein, and other non-Christians. I may even see Jesus there, for he was a Jew, not a Christian.

Unfortunately, many Christians have abused—and still do—the teachings of Jesus and distort the Bible for their own ends. I find it incredible that the message of a carpenter, who taught us to love others as we do ourselves, could have become so distorted. Perhaps I shouldn't be so surprised. Two people who did much to spread the word of his teachings were both murderers. The first Christian Roman emperor, Constantine, killed his own family, and John Calvin murdered Michael Servetus because he disagreed with him about the Trinity. Mercy was not a word high on the agenda of these forefathers of the Church. They laid down the law for their own personal power. For many years, everything advocated in the Bible was considered as coming from God. For example, during the days of slavery, members of the clergy—and others—held stock in slave ships and slave-trading concerns, and they justified this by quoting biblical texts.

The literature that sums up all the best ideas about hell is perhaps Dante Alighieri's *Divine Comedy*, which was published in the fourteenth century. (I mentioned him earlier in relation to suicides.) Many readers of this epic poem actually believed that Dante had made the trip to hell and back. In the story, Dante finds himself lost in a dark forest where he is rescued by his literary hero, the Roman poet Virgil. Virgil tells Dante that he is looking for Beatrice—his lost love who awaits him in heaven. (Dante's own first love was also called Beatrice, and she died during childhood.) Virgil's mission is to guide Dante to her. The journey will take them through hell and purgatory.

Assuming that Dante got it right, here are a few of the things that you can do if you go to hell or purgatory:

Give up hope. Instead of a welcome mat, hell has written across its gates the words "Abandon Hope All Ye Who Enter Here." This is UTTER ruin, eternal damnation, permanent perdition. Hopefully humming a tune, wishfully whistling, and assured smiling are forbidden.

Take a boat trip. Outings with the grim boatman Charon are popular all year round. Take a trip with other dammed souls across the river Acheron to the Inferno. Unfortunately, the crossing is usually pretty choppy there, and the sulphurous odors can be a little distracting.

Play ball games. This one is only for hoarders, squanderers, and those who have sinned through greed. These people are doomed forever to roll massive boulders against each other. A useful tip is to not pay the boatman, and you'll get in for free.

Windsurf. Again admittance is restricted. This one is only for people who are lustful. You can join in anytime—24/7. It's even open Christmas Day. You will be perpetually tossed and whirled in hurricane winds. This activity particularly attracts some well-known souls. Dante spotted Cleopatra, Helen of Troy, and Helen's lover Paris.

Roast marshmallows. My personal favorite, this section of hell is reserved for heretics. Accommodation is, however, a little cramped. You will be given your own fiery tomb on the vast plain within the walled city of Dis in nether hell.

Take a woodland tour. Actually you don't get to see much on this excursion. For those of you who have taken your own life, you will be transformed into a grotesque tree. Because you rejected life on earth, you will now stand fixed and withered in hell.

Play the amusements. This one's popular with the clergy. Faithless priests who use their position within the church to gain temporal wealth are condemned to spend eternity upside down in reeking holes.

Visit the reptile house. You may need to take someone else's ticket in order to get in. This place is for thieves, who are then eternally crushed by monstrous snakes.

Enjoy the magic show. You don't need to volunteer, for participation in the show is mandatory. Here, sowers of discord among families, churches, and nations are doomed to be continually split apart by a sword-wielding demon. Cuts are perpetually healed and reopened so that the fun can last indefinitely.

Play winter games. This is the in-house favorite of the residents and the resting place of the Devil, who spends his time chewing on the head of Judas Iscariot. Here the giant Antaeus will personally lower you into the frozen lake that fills the Pit of Hell. Icebound in the silent Lake Cocytus reside the traitors to country and betrayers of family.

Marvel at the freak show. Popular with the kids is the scary sight of the woman Arcane, who was transformed into a spider for the sin of pride. You are likely to meet many of my personal friends here. You will recognize them, for their heads have been twisted around to look forever behind them as punishment for the sin of foretelling the future. I predict you will want to go there.

You'll be glad to know that Dante eventually ascends to Paradise . . . and gets the girl.

THE REAL HELL

Hell is usually depicted as punishment and retribution for sin. Within many religions, it is described as eternal damnation. When you go to hell, it's a one-way ticket—there's no coming back. Commit a sin in this life—such as not believing in the doctrines of your church—and it's down to the sulphurous pits for you. You will be damned forever. The only way to avoid your diabolical destiny is to conform to what you are told by your religious leaders.

It will probably come as no surprise to hear that I don't believe in hell and eternal punishment. It just doesn't square with what I understand from my own mediumistic work and the spiritual insights of others. In particular, I have been inspired by my correspondence with Victor Zammit, a retired Australian attorney who argues in his book *A Lawyer Presents the Case for the Afterlife* that there is objective evidence for the existence of the afterlife. Indeed he says: "I have come to the irreversible conclusion that there is a great body of evidence which, taken *as a whole*, absolutely and without a doubt proves the case for the afterlife." Victor Zammit presents such a solid case that he offers a million dollars on his website www.victorzammit.com to any afterlife researcher who can rebut the existing evidence for the afterlife. So far James Randi and other well-known skeptics have not taken up the challenge.

I was intrigued by Victor's position regarding a case for the existence of hell, purgatory, and judgment day. "Hell for eternity and eternal damnation were invented by men to manipulate the hearts and minds of the unaware—they do NOT exist. Whilst there ARE lower spheres in the afterlife that are particularly dark, unpleasant and even horrific—some call them 'hell'—ending down there is not for eternity. There is always help available for any soul willing to learn the lessons of kindness and unselfishness."

It is clear that not every person is worthy of the same treatment in the next world. I wholeheartedly agree with Victor Zammit that hell for eternity was invented by human beings to manipulate the hearts and minds of the unaware. Nonetheless, there certainly are lower spheres in the afterlife. For some, it may be experienced like the classic depictions of hell, but it is not forever. This place, like the higher levels, is there to help you grow. Spiritualist mediums follow a set of seven principles, one of which states that there is "eternal progress open to every human soul"— meaning that everyone, no matter how far they may fall, will eventually progress to the divine realms.

It is our ability to love, not faith, that determines our progress in the beyond. Religious belief is of little use to you unless you have embraced the spiritual principles behind your religion, put it into practice in your earthly life, and made it part of you. In other words, unless you have grown to become a truly spiritual person and not just someone who pays lip service to other people's ideas. I would personally much rather burn in hell with the likes of Ghandi and Socrates than live an eternity with religious bigots. Clearly it is not religious beliefs that form a person's character but their application of spiritual values. Atheists, agnostics, and skeptics will fare just as well as anyone else so long as at heart they are a decent person.

Ignorance, egotism, aversion, attachment, and clinging to life are the five most common causes of suffering in both this world and the next. Most of us resist life, we refuse to flow with changes that happen or accept things as they are. We say no to life and an even bigger NO to death. But if we live and die with a spirit of acceptance and trust in the fact that there is an ever-present divine flow working unseen in the background of our lives; if we simply surrender to the divine that is even now unfolding in our heart and have enough trust to flow with it, then we will certainly arrive safely at the next shore.

It is resistance that creates a hell within ourselves and can make a hell of earthly life. This same spiritual resistance can pull us into the hell state after death. Departed souls, who in their earthly lives were dogmatic, had fixed ideas, imperious views, or blinkered beliefs are most likely to run into difficulties at the time of death. They will resist the inevitability of death and cannot flow with the new conditions and reality they find beyond the veil. Even at the moment of physical death, bigotry and mental preconceptions can slow the vibration of the subtle body and make the release from the material plane more difficult. This is why so many cultures say prayers over the dead to remind the listening soul of the greater purpose of their existence and to encourage them to seek refuge in the next world.

We want them to progress, to let go of earthly life and find life anew in the next world.

For the bereaved of all cultures, it is imperative that the departing soul moves on, that they do not cling to earthly life or worse still be pulled into any form of afterlife suffering. For those who on earth were deeply caught in negative habits and vices may get caught on a lower astral level and not be able to progress until the habits are completely removed or they are drawn toward another earthly incarnation.

Most people when they die are met by their loved ones, their spiritual guardians, and beings who are part of their group soul. People who have been scoundrels in life may find themselves alone or greeted by other dark souls with a similar nature to their own. Together they will be drawn into the shadowy lower spheres. Similarly, the negative karma that such persons have accumulated while in life now pulls them like a heavy weight into these dark worlds. Lies, greed, cheating, and cruelty to others hang upon them like morbid, heavy weights and pull them into places where they will be forced to confront the consequences of their deeds. Deathbed confessions or baptisms make no difference. You are what you are, and this determines the life to come.

THE DREAM OF THE SOUL

Hell, like heaven, has many different planes. In fact, it is not somewhere separate from heaven. There is no demarcation between heaven and hell—they are degrees of the one same reality. The degree of hell-like quality is determined by the person's own nature.

People who are overtly wicked may immediately find themselves in a terrible place. It may not be a place where devils poke you with tridents, but may feel much the same. For example, a corrupt doctor from the German death camps of WWII may find himself experiencing the same horrors that were inflicted on his victims on earth. The afterworld of such souls will be like a nightmare that has become reality. But far worse than this will be the realization of what he or she has done. The angelic beings will present the culprits to their victims, who were made to suffer. They will feel every drop of pain that was inflicted upon their victims—from both the spirit worlds and from those still alive on earth. And this will not be a momentary experience but one which will afflict them until such time as they want to reform themselves.

We can only rise to the highest spheres if we vibrate with love. During our earthly life an inner alchemy takes place in the soul of a person who has good intent. The love we feel and the good we do both in thought and deed quicken our vibration so that on death we can rise to the higher spheres. It is our capacity to love that gives us entry to the blissful realms. Most people will go directly to one of these higher spheres, too beautiful to imagine, or elect to experience worlds almost the same as the earth plane. These are the realms of light. However, because we have come to terms with the negative sides of our own natures, we "descend" to the more earth-like realms to resolve those negative aspects.

Similarly, there may be realms in the beyond where life from other faraway planets can resolve their karma in surroundings that are familiar to them. Initially they too will experience the same realm of light that is the common heritage for all life. But, just like us, they may need to descend to worlds that are similar to those they left behind after death. It is my understanding that each planetary group remains within its own heavenly realm. Perhaps it is possible for alien life and human life to share a similar world in the afterlife. However, this we cannot know for certain, as there has been no empirical proof so far to support the fact that aliens can communicate through human mediums. What I have witnessed thus far is highly suspect. Nonetheless, perhaps the time will come when alien contact via the afterlife plane will provide proof of their existence. It would require, however, some verifiable evidence, perhaps a scientific fact that has yet eluded our most advanced scientific technology and minds.

Human or nonhuman, your bad qualities will, at times, cause you to experience personal hells, generating scenarios in which you are able to consider issues in your life. For example, suppose you went through a divorce, with all of its hurtful aggression and legalized nastiness. Suddenly, you experience details of it again, but from the perspective of your ex-partner. Similarly, if you've willingly done things to hurt another, you may find your roles now reversed. The afterlife is a bit like virtual dreaming, which the soul can use to generate scenarios designed to enlighten. These dreams may be "good" or "bad," but this is not about reward and punishment. It's part of the road to be traveled to attain spiritual reform and growth.

The afterlife planes are a continuation of the process of the life review, except now they are played out like a cosmic play. The good and bad deeds done on earth set the themes. Fortunately, there is always a happy ending to the cosmic play, for every sentient being will eventually know the bliss of the infinite even though, for some, this may take the work of many earth lives and extended periods spent in study and contemplation on different levels of the afterlife worlds.

SPIRITUAL REFORM

There are places in the next life where every man, woman, and child actively tries to inflict as much emotional pain as possible on everyone else there. When they died, they were drawn together into these levels like a magnet. People of a similar disposition are drawn together by their makeup. There are places for thieves, pedophiles, murderers, liars, sadists, and the greedy. There are millions of hells.

I have been told by the spirit people that hell is not a place to be feared but a state of being that is necessary for some souls to grow toward the light. For example, on one occasion I worked with a group of mediums to "clear" a spirit that was causing poltergeist activity on board a boat. When the spirit spoke to us, through one of the mediums, we learned that the spirit was not moving on to the next world because he feared punishment for a crime he had committed while on earth. So, he was "clinging" to the aura of the woman now living in the cabin in which he had once lived. The solution was to get him to connect with his angelic helper and those in the spirit world who loved him. When he finally did so, he let go of his paralyzing fear and moved toward the light—and no longer troubled the boat's passengers. It was his fear of what he believed awaited him in hell that prevented his moving on to the next world.

Soon after this, one of the mediums involved was given a message from the spirit who had caused the poltergeist activity. He was now happy in the afterlife; his irrational fear of a personal hell had been one of ignorance. He was not being punished so much as being helped to come to terms with what had happened and caused his distress.

I recall another incident in which a spirit told us that he had done terrible things while on earth. He had spent much time in the lower planes facing the wrongs he had done. Now he had progressed from that place and wanted to help others to know that God's world can be opened up even to the most hardened sinner as long as he or she is willing to reform. This spirit now works in helping other mediums. When he shows himself to clairvoyant people, they see him as wearing a Nazi uniform.

The highly respected American doctor Carl A. Wickland recorded some very interesting cases of spirits who spoke through his wife's trance mediumship during the 1920s. In some instances, criminals spoke to the group and explained what happens to criminals when they die. In one instance, the spirit of a hanged criminal named Pete Neidemeyer spoke to the Wickland's Spiritualist circle to tell what happened to him after death:

"The first thing I had to do was to conquer self, and it is very hard to conquer selfishness when you have never thought of anything else but selfishness. We must conquer that before we can do any work in the spirit world.

"The best way is to be put in a dark room—we sometimes call it a dungeon—where we see nothing but ourselves and our acts of the past. One after another these acts come crowding in. The good ones are so few that they hardly count for anything. When we do see a good act, it seems as if it belongs to someone else. We have to stay there until our hearts and our eyes are opened. When we seek to overcome our bad habits and to live for others, then we get out of the selfish state.

"My heart was very hardened, but finally I cried out: 'Not my will any longer, but thine.'

"The first thing to be done is to help the very lowest we come in contact with. I felt that I did not want to assist with this or that, but I had to. I had to learn patience. When we can serve without grumbling and do it for the love of our fellow man, it does not seem so hard.

"So I have gone on from one thing to another, always learning, and through learning I have stepped into a more beautiful condition. In the invisible world we advance by stages, but only through learning."

ESCAPING THE LOWER PLANES

There are also planes of hell where the inhabitants are so wrapped up in their own wickedness that they are hardly aware of the existence of the worlds of light that most people will know in the life beyond death. These spiritually lower planes are filled with the darkness of hate and draw only the worst of people. Here reside those now subhuman spirits who, instead of striving for enlightenment, have descended into a demonic state of being. Although once human, they have now become caricatures of their own evil. Even here, however, there is the option of redemption.

We create our own personal hell—not a form of punishment but self-created in order to resolve our imperfections. As this happens, the burdens on the soul become lighter and allow it to move "upward" to the paradise planes of the afterlife. Only through the process of spiritual development can the soul escape the weight of the karma that prevents it from rising to the higher planes of the afterlife. (Strictly speaking, it is all about change of vibration rate rather than any "up" or "down" direction to heaven or to hell.)

For centuries, religions have used the concept of hell to frighten people into subscribing to their belief system. Mediums have been condemned to death as witches and warlocks and subjected to all sorts of horrible tortures. Their bodies were buried in unhallowed ground with knives and rivets through the thighs, knee bones, and feet to prevent the corpse from later rising and walking. Since 1712, when the last witch was burned in England, mediumship has developed and shown us that the hell planes are only a temporary sojourn on the soul's journey. Also, we have learned, through mediumship, that the angelic beings are able to descend to hell in order to help guide the souls who are there toward a better way of living. Even in this terrible level of being, God's work goes on.

THE ANGELIC REALMS

"Good night, sweet prince, and flights of angels sing thee to thy rest!"

—WILLIAM SHAKESPEARE
(HORATIO SPEAKING TO THE DEAD HAMLET)

❧

ANGELS HAVE EXISTED SINCE the dawn of creation, in every culture, myth, and tradition. They are normally portrayed as being filled with grace and beauty and represent a higher order than humankind. The word "angel" in Greek means "messenger," and they are considered to be intermediaries between the Creator and the created, the bridge between heaven and earth. In both the Old and New Testaments of the Bible, angels are the primary divine messengers through whom God communicates with humankind. Angels bring their messages to people on earth and also to the people in the afterlife.

A belief in angels existed in very ancient civilizations. For example, angels are depicted in carvings from Babylon that date between 2500 and 1000 B.C.E., and some archaeologists claim that the tradition dates back even much further. References to angel-like beings can also be found in shaman lore and within tribal societies.

Angels are considered to be the guardians of the soul, continuingly trying to inspire us to live a life that is happy, harmonious, and fulfilling. In early Judeo-Christian theology, the Angel of Repentance reminded humans of their sins and offered opportunities for forgiveness. It is said that, after death, the Angel of Peace carried worthy souls to the heavenly planes. Individuals each have a personal angel, guardian of his or her soul, who will be present at the judgment of the soul after death. Similar traditions can be found in Islamic beliefs. For example, the prophet Mohammed received the words of the Qur'an from the angel Gabriel. Angels have been expressed in art and written about through the ages.

The appearance of wings in many of the depictions of angels is merely to portray their "flight" between heaven and earth. Call it artistic license, but it serves as a reminder that they are not of this earth plane. If you encounter angels in the afterlife, they may not necessarily appear to you in their traditional guise. Angels, when required to take a form, will assume the likeness of that which is held in the person's consciousness to whom they are appearing: to some, a male/female figure; to others, simply a ball of light. (In my book *The Psychic Casebook*, I explain how an angel visited my wife and me. It appeared in the room as a brilliant ball of light, floating about six feet in front of us. This was not clairvoyant vision or shared hallucination, it was undeniably real.)

Most traditions claim that angels have never taken human birth, that they are a different state of being from us entirely. Angels are genderless; although they have male- or female-type energies. They are exactly that: energy or spirit. The contemporary American philosopher Mortimer Adler postulates that angels are minds without bodies and take human form only as part of their earth ministry. Once their given task is finished, they return to the afterlife and shed every last vestige of corporeality. Others say that angels may be considered superior to humans, because they know that their true essence is love, whereas humans have forgotten that their divine heredity is love.

Speculation about the nature of angels thrived in the Middle Ages, and to this day many people believe that angels have influenced their lives. Although there are different opinions as to their rank, names, and station, angels are said to have a hierarchy. The most influential theories about angels were put forward in the eleventh century by the philosopher Thomas Aquinas, who enjoyed being known as the Angelic Doctor. He believed that angels were "all intellect," totally without matter. Aquinas proposed that the angelic worlds consisted of orders (or "choirs") split into groups of three, each group of three forming what is called a *triad*. The first triad is the nearest to God, and the last nearest to man.

The first triad consists of Seraphim, Cherubim, and Ophanim. They are the closest to God and are keepers of divine love and wisdom.

The second triad, below the first triad, has the function of maintaining a pivot between those nearest to God and those nearest to man. They are called the Dominions, Virtues, and Powers.

The final triad consists of the Principalities, Archangels, and Angels. These work closest to humans. Most angels have "el" in their name, meaning "of God." The four most recognized of the archangels are Michael, Gabriel, Raphael, and Uriel; each represents a season, direction, and element.

My own feeling about angels—a view that has been expressed by other mediums—is that they are beings from the higher realms of being. Some of these angels were once human, and it is the objective of human existence to become angelic ourselves. Angels are the souls of those who never need to come back to the earth plane again. The joy of their work is to open closed minds and to soften hard hearts. They come sometimes to help those who lack compassion, understanding, and forgiveness by filling their hearts with faith, love, and trust.

One day we will all become like angels.

RELATIONSHIPS

"I know that I'm going where Lucy is."

—Rutherford B. Hayes

SOUL MATES

In the past, illness, war, and poverty were the main causes of worry for most people. Today the world has changed, and modern people's main worries have turned more toward human relationships. We still have the old difficulties, of course, and lots of new ones—particularly stress-related and close-quarter illnesses that come with city life. Troubled relationships, nonetheless, are high on most people's do-something-about list in striving for happiness.

My spiritual work is primarily to help the bereaved, but I sometimes also find myself helping people with their life issues. At the top of that list, and by far the cause of more mental anguish than anything else, are relationship problems. There are, however, a few wonderful exceptions. For example, one client named Sarah told me that for years she had a recurring dream of the same man. "The dream has been with me ever since I was a kid," Sarah explained. "I knew every detail about him. His name was Paul, he had dark hair, and he was in the Navy."

Then Sarah met her dream lover at a nightclub. "Everything about Paul was exactly the same as in my dream," continued Sarah. "Yes, he was in the Navy, and he had dark hair. But in the dream he hands me a red rose and a white silk scarf." What happened next, as Sarah related it, "Paul told me of his recurring dreams. In them he gives a woman—who looks exactly like me—a red rose and silk scarf!"

It would appear that Paul and Sarah were destined to be together, having been dreaming of each other from an early age. The last that I heard was that they are now planning to get married.

A similar predetermination happened to me. The famous psychic medium Doris Stokes told me that I'd meet my future wife, Jane Wallis, on the 6th of March. She was slightly wrong. I met and soon married Jane Willis on the 6th of March, 1989.

Do you feel that there is another person who is your ideal partner and with whom you have a preexisting spiritual bond? If that person has not incarnated or has passed on earlier in life, your search could last a lifetime. It's possible, though, that your paths simply have not crossed, or that they did but you did not recognize each other. Perhaps you will only discover who your soul mate is after returning to the afterlife.

Some occult traditions state that the soul is really hermaphroditic: that far back in time each soul split into two parts, male and female, and that the souls of the two half-beings will eventually become one again. In psychological terms, it may result from the need for our own spiritual wholeness. Carl Jung claimed that each of us is psychologically part male and part female. He called these two aspects of the self the *Anima* (female) and the *Animus* (male). The Anima and Animus appear in dreams and fantasies as the perfect man or woman. They are often projected onto the opposite sex, resulting in the experience of "falling in love." During dreams, the figures manifest as a guide to the soul and offer creative possibilities for the individuation process. It could be argued that the romantic notion of a soul mate occurs because modern people have failed to instigate the inner quest toward spiritual wholeness. This inner process is now projected onto other people, whom we see as the antidote for all our troubles.

Some people believe that soul mates are two halves of one soul that has been split apart to speed up the process of spiritual evolution by taking in earth-plane experiences at double speed. In this instance, finding one's soul mate is literally finding one's other half. I see no reason why the soul has to evolve at rapid speed; as it has already spent millions of years getting to the point we are at now. Similarly, human relations are never perfect, and even soul mates need to argue and go through the trials that all relationships tend to encounter at some time. It's all part of a healthy relationship. It's our differences that push us emotionally and spiritually forward. Soul mates is clearly an appealing romantic notion, but I am uncertain whether it is a reality.

Nonetheless, we sometimes meet people in life whom we instantly like or dislike. This can apply to friends as well as to persons we fall in love with or marry. There are also powerful bonds between families and occasionally between groups of friends. Could it be that some souls are interconnected by an invisible affiliation? Is there perhaps a coming together of souls that some have called the *group soul*?

THE GROUP SOUL

"You have been mine before,—How long ago I may not know:
But just when at that swallow's soar
Your neck turn'd so,
Some veil did fall,—I knew it all of yore."
—DANTE GABRIEL ROSSETTI (1828–1882)

❧

MY SPIRITUAL GUIDE HAS TOLD my group that only a part of an individual's identity incarnates at any one time. Like a diamond with many facets, only one face is turned to the world. Part of us exists here, on the earth plane, and there's another part that is not born at all. It remains in the afterlife. By centering our awareness on this part of ourselves, we can become aware of the afterlife itself. Mediumship is, in effect, introspection.

During your normal life, you may notice that your consciousness is continually shifting. It is as if it is moving up and down a ladder. For example, there may be times when you are filled with spiritual feelings and are unattached to the ties of the world. However, at other times, you may be filled with anger and other such negative emotions, and your consciousness is far from spiritual. Often people we think of as spiritual can show traits that contradict this. In all of us there is both the serene, enlightened being and the animalistic "monkey mind" (a term used in the East to describe the lower self).

We are continually moving up and down the ladder of our being. The objective of human spiritual development is to establish habits that enable us to move up the ladder and remain centered in our spiritual self. The "monkey mind" is difficult to transcend. Just like a monkey, it is easily distracted and can sometimes be sneaky and tricky. It is the aspect of ourselves that creates the ego that clings to selfishness and self-importance. It takes itself very seriously and is very much bound to earthly life.

In the afterlife, we continue to move up and down the ladder of consciousness. However, now this movement becomes more apparent to us. For example, on earth the world may not look especially bright when we are in a glum mood but, in the mental worlds of the afterlife, the whole environment alters according to our state of mind. As our center of consciousness changes, so does the world around us.

The "monkey mind" likes to put itself first. The "enlightened mind" puts others first. Most of us fall somewhere in between these conditions. When self becomes less important to us, we can move toward the "enlightened mind." And when we do this, we discover that we are all fundamentally the same. The innermost part of us, from which everything else about us has arisen, remains unborn. It is at one with God. By knowing in essence this, we can know everything, for everything has arisen from this one source.

Some mystical systems also talk of the "oversoul" or "overself." This is the real "I" that manages us from a higher plane of existence. In Sanskrit it is called the *Adhyatma* and is the nucleus of the higher self. Michael Newton, Ph.D., who has spoken to the spirits using hypnosis, explains it as the link with all souls to its existence. "All souls are part of the same divine essence, generated from one oversoul. This intelligent energy is universal in scope and so we all share in divine status. If our soul reflects a small portion of the oversoul we call God, then our guides provide the mirror by which we are able to see ourselves connected to this creator."

I have often wondered if the guides are part of the overself, but questions put to my guide when I am in trance indicate that the guide has an independent existence. Starting at the top of the ladder of being, we can say that all things belong to the one group soul. As this innocent soul subdivides in order to gain experience and self-knowledge, it forms many other souls. Just as stars form into galaxies, so souls are attracted together into groups. We are members of the earth soul group. There are also soul groups for alien species.

ALIEN GROUP SOULS

Asked whether we can link to beings of the alien group souls, my spiritual guides have explained that it is of no benefit. Just as there is a vast distance between the galaxies, so too is there a division between the spiritual states of each system. In the highest realms, we can become aware of each other; but this is "no big deal" as they say, as by this time we have attained the same spiritual state and therefore know the same things. Seeking out alien beings through mediumship is a distraction and subject to fantasy. It is better to seek out direct experience of the spiritual states of being to which all life attains.

I had a somewhat off-putting experience of alien trance mediumship. I was invited to attend a small group, doing some very interesting work with past-life regression hypnotism. Here I saw some very interesting stuff, including witnessing someone I knew speaking Old French—even though they had no knowledge of the language. Toward the end of the evening, one of the visitors said she would like to demonstrate how to channel aliens. This would not be a hypnotic demonstration. She proudly explained that, in this, she was far higher than any medium: she was a "natural."

Maybe it was the squeaky high voice, or perhaps the opening words "We come in peace," that put me off. The host and I squirmed with embarrassment as we listened to some of the most amazing nonsense ever heard. Everything was completely unsubstantiated by any facts that could be verified, but spoken with great authority. The worrying part was that others in the room were taking it seriously. We had listened to a wonderful demonstration of the "monkey mind" in action.

YOUR GROUP SOUL

It may be that certain souls belong to a group of souls that are like many parts of one being—similar in some way to how a swarm of bees appears to have a consciousness of its own, or a crowd of people act as if with one mind. The group soul may be a form of shared consciousness, originating from the earliest spirit formation. Evolving over many animal lifetimes, this soul group then likely began to share human incarnations together. If this is the case, then many of the people you know and love may be part of the same soul group.

When we progress to the higher realms of the spirit, individual identity becomes less important, and we gradually merge again with the members of our group. This process continues with your group soul merging with other group souls, ad infinitum. Eventually all souls merge together as one.

My own feeling about this is that all life is interconnected in some way, and this interconnectedness extends through all levels of life and death (a bit like the "force" alluded to in the movie *Star Wars*). However, I do feel that individual will is important. We are all a unique expression of God's nature.

We have a certain affiliation with some people because we have spent time with each other over many incarnations. I believe that because of this we return together in groups. This may be why certain families—such as the Kennedys—may have a family karma. The idea here is that, because of karmic involvement from past lives, we may return together to reap the effects of these past interactions. According to this view, fathers and sons, for example, might reverse roles in successive lifetimes in order to balance the karmic debt.

We are like small bands of traveling players that come together to act out a play that we planned while in the afterlife, actually between-life, planes. Sometimes we swap roles, and occasionally a new player joins the group for a while. The costumes change, the sets are different, and the story's themes are altered, but most of the actors and actresses remain the same.

THE ASSEMBLY OF THE GROUP SOUL

When you join the afterlife, you will recognize the people who are a part of your group soul. Many of these people will have moved to the afterlife before you, and others will still be walking the earth. Some may not have incarnated with you this time around, but you will nonetheless recognize them from time long past. Your kinship is such that it will feel as if no time has passed. Just like when you meet a close friend from years ago, and it is as if not more than a day has passed since you last spoke. You carry on where you left off.

You will spend a great deal of your time in the afterlife interacting with these people to whom you have a soul resonance, and the decision to reincarnate will be decided collectively among you. Although you may not initially all be born into the same family, or close to one another, the natural law will ensure that eventually your paths will meet, and you will share new experiences together. Among the people of your group soul will be those you love and those you may need in order to share and overcome future challenges.

THE GREAT WHEEL OF BIRTH AND DEATH

"He who binds to himself a joy
Does the winged life destroy;
But he who kisses the joy as it flies
Lives in eternity's sunrise."

—WILLIAM BLAKE (1757–1827)

REINCARNATION IS THE PROGRESS of the soul through many lives. It enables you to grow to your full potential and eventually attain cosmic consciousness. The earth is the schoolhouse where we come to learn our lessons. We live many lives on earth, just as we go through many grades in a school before we graduate. Walking among us are many souls at different stages of development. Some have been here many times before, whereas for others, this is their first lesson in a human incarnation. We graduate when our spirituality is developed enough so that we no longer need a physical body to continue our spiritual work.

The problem with earthly life is that it is easy to become spiritually lost and forget the reason we came here. Every time we come to earth, we develop new imperfections and new desires. These desires draw us back to the earth plane until they are fulfilled, or we attain enough wisdom to let go of them. As the Buddha has explained, these desires are the cause of our suffering because we cling to them, yet they can never be gratified. It is the nature of desire that each time one "satisfies" it, the craving to repeat the experience returns. In this way we become trapped in an eternal wheel of desire and the satisfaction of desire.

Sigmund Freud has shown us, however, that the repression of desire, particularly sexual desire, can be unhealthful and in some cases lead to serious psychological problems. If we force desire from our consciousness, then otherwise small desires will return in a stronger way. Persistent repression will create anxieties and odd behavior. The Eastern way is to let go of desire rather than repress these forces. For example, the best way to stop smoking is to gently let go of the craving rather than wrestle with the problem and thereby increase its grip on you. Yoga teaches us to root out bad, selfish habits and replace them with good ones. With this gentle self-discipline, we gradually free ourselves from craving and eventually from the animalistic desires that can chain us to earthly incarnations.

People who have used their earthly life for spiritual progress and to emulate great men and women find it much easier to adjust to the next world, and they can progress to the higher planes of being. Similarly, when the time comes to return to earth for more experience, they have a greater degree of choice about the life they will lead. Instead of being drawn by the need to gratify desire, they make conscious choices based upon what they know to be best for the soul.

Most of us are not saints or hedonists. Our path falls somewhere between the two extremes. We are sometimes motivated by our desires, but also have a degree of control. In the final analysis, it's "who we are" that decides the path ahead. At the beginning of this book, I explained how our character today will determine what happens to us after death. Similarly, our character also determines the new birth we shall take when our time in the afterlife has concluded. The wonderful thing about all of this is that whatever happens to us in this material life, in the afterlife, or in future incarnations, it is all under our control. We can have a better future simply by becoming a better person.

You will carry your present state into the next life and not become an angel just because you die. Unless you have used some of your earthly life to quicken the spirit, you will not progress. However, if you use your time on earth to conquer yourself and improve your nature, you will achieve a better state in the afterlife and an auspicious birth when the time comes to reincarnate. This is why earthly life is so important. In a human incarnation, we are given the opportunity to make great spiritual progress. Better to check your words, actions, thoughts, character, and heart than to waste a life in pursuit of ephemeral earthly goals. This life is a spiritual opportunity.

As the time approaches for you to reincarnate, you will begin to feel an increasing attachment to your natural tendencies. For example, if you were a powerful person in your previous incarnation, you may be filled now with a feeling of ambition. You may also feel a tendency toward certain sensations. If you lived in a tropical climate, you may be drawn to incarnate in a hot place again or to seek out its opposite. If, for example, you lived a life as a seaman, you may again be drawn to incarnate near an ocean. You may be drawn to incarnate in a situation that provides you with the opportunity to fulfill creative desires unfulfilled in past lives or to apply new things discovered while in the spirit world.

Sometimes people incarnate almost immediately after death and do not get the opportunity for self-healing and reflection that the afterlife provides. Their bodies may show physical marks that hint at what happened to cause this instantaneous rebirth. For example, I have met people who believe they were burned as witches in their former life. Today they suffer from skin complaints. The most evidential proof for reincarnation comes from people who have been reborn within a generation and have met friends and family from their former life. In these cases, the memory of the former life remains fresh.

In future lives, you may have hazy memories of this life. If today you live in New York, you may in your next life want to be born in the bustle of the metropolis of the future. If you live in Alaska, you may seek a life of adventure exploring the cold reaches of outer space. Maybe, at some distant date, you will recall dim memories of America as it was in the twenty-first century, in the days before global warming, when you could walk outdoors without protective clothing.

PREPARING FOR REBIRTH

"The woods are lovely, dark and deep.
But I have promises to keep,
And miles to go before I sleep,
And miles to go before I sleep."

—ROBERT FROST (1874–1963)

YOUR UNFULFILLED DESIRE WILL draw you once again to the earth. Your heart holds a promise to yourself and to God to develop your spirituality. Your time spent in the afterlife has refreshed you and now gives you the vitality and enthusiasm you need to again journey the paths of life. The pull toward the earth is irresistible, just as the pull toward the afterlife was irresistible when you left your body. And just as you were guided toward death by your guardian angels, so they return now to guide you to your new earthly life.

A blueprint for your new life will unfold as your tendencies manifest and you recognize the needs of your soul. The path you plan may not be one of all joy. Your outline for the future will include opportunities for happiness, but also opportunities for suffering. Together with your guardians, you will look for the combination of qualities that will enable you to spiritually evolve. In addition, your future life will be designed to share a common destiny with the people from your group soul.

The above procedure sounds very complicated, but it is, in fact, a spontaneous process. The blueprint for your destiny is subject to natural law. The details manifest according to the karma to be actualized and the love you have for others. Love seeks itself. Because of this, the people you love incarnate along with you to continue and advance the story of your group soul. Similarly, the people you have had problems with in your past life may be drawn into your life again, so that the difficulties can be resolved and you learn the lesson of forgiveness. For example, a troublesome ex-partner may incarnate as one of your children.

When the moment comes for you to be born, you will again be drawn into the light of the divine. Just as when you entered the afterlife you became aware of the greater purpose of your life and were asked if you were ready to die, now you are asked if you are ready to be born. This will happen on an abstract level that is impossible to describe. The closest simile is that you merge with the light and momentarily become one with God. You have free will, but will inevitably accept your new birth unconditionally. You will see that, suffering included, it is the right path to take—one that will bring you, eventually, to a happy completeness.

When you are ready, you will let go of all your memories of your previous life (the one you are living now as you read this book) and of your time in the afterlife. You will accept that this is necessary and understand that you will regain all of these memories when you return to the afterlife the next time you die. You will recognize that life is an ever-changing show, made up of different acts. With each incarnation, you are given another chance. By forgetting your previous lives, your baggage drops away from you. The slate is wiped clean. However, those with whom you have shared love in previous lifetimes will be drawn to you by the power of natural law, so that your love can be perfected. Our memories of one another, however, are clouded for a time so that we do not become clannish and are more easily able to expand our love to include new people, eventually realizing that all is one in love.

You will forget the universal knowledge before you return to the life of the body. One of the first stories about this comes from the ancient Greek philosopher Plato, who, in *The Republic,* records the experiences of a soldier named Er, who was allowed to return from death. He is, perhaps, the first recorded case of a near-death experience.

Er describes how the souls who were allowed to return to earth had to first drink of the waters of the River of Forgetfulness. Some of them, "who were not saved by good sense," drank too much. Er was fortunate enough to remember his visit to the afterlife as he awoke, on his funeral pyre just before it was to be set alight! It is interesting that, even in this early account, the forgetting is shown to be voluntary.

With your memory now gone, or greatly diminished, you return to the earth, tumbling again down the tunnel of light. Gradually, you lose consciousness and slip into a deep, sleep-like state, ready to slowly awaken in the waters of your new mother's womb.

THE CAUSAL WORLD

"And if you enter the theatre as you are, you would see everything through the eyes of Harry and the old spectacles of the Steppenwolf. You are therefore requested to lay these spectacles aside and to be so kind as to leave your highly esteemed personality here in the cloak-room, where you will find it again when you wish."

—HERMANN HESSE (FROM *Steppenwolf*)

THE DESCRIPTIONS OF THE afterlife that we have considered all relate to a world of form. In many ways, the states described are an exalted continuation of the experiences of earth. However, is there a state of being that goes beyond all of this? Could there be a final resting-place for the soul from which we return no more? A place where incarnations are no longer necessary?

To some people, enjoying an existence in heaven is the highest aim of life. However, there is a state of being that transcends even the celestial pleasures and is eternal. It is without beginning and endless. The understanding of this can only come when you finally merge with the Absolute—into a state that may also be called God.

The cycles of birth and death help you to attain perfection gradually, through experience. The positive karma accumulated during a lifetime secures for you time in the afterlife. Our experience in life, however, shows that whatever we consider pleasure is always accompanied by some sort of pain. Pleasure and pain could not exist without one another. If pleasure were to continue forever, it would not be pleasure at all. Without its opposite, we would be unable to enjoy pleasure. Every kind of earthly pleasure is related to some form of pain or suffering. And so it is in the heavenly world.

On the earth plane, the duration of suffering is longer than the duration of pleasure. In the heavenly planes, the reverse is true: pleasure is long and pain is limited. However, an eternity spent in this state of being would eventually become monotonous, because the celestial pleasures are also limited by time and space. Because of this, pleasure also cannot be eternal. Your good thoughts and good deeds will take you to the heavenly realms, but these by themselves are not enough to sustain indefinitely, and you are drawn back to be reborn.

Just as I spoke about how attachment to the material world and the body can stop our progressing upward, so too does attachment to the celestial worlds hold us back from our ultimate goal. A point will come when you will want to transcend even the joy of heaven. You will yearn to join a higher cosmic plane from which nobody returns, and you need never incarnate, or take physical form, again.

This higher plane of existence is often called the *causal planes*; called *Brahmaloka* by the Hindus. Eventually, you will even leave this blissful plane, and unite forever with the omnipresent God.

THE SECOND DEATH

In the causal plane, everything is reduced to its essence. Nothing is lost. Everything you are and have been is retained. However, the manifestation of a body or an environment will become less important. You will truly become aware that you are a being of light. You will not necessarily have a bodily form, but become as pure light. Your consciousness will no longer need form.

These states of being are impossible for us to fully comprehend while we reside in the world of form. Perhaps the best synonym is to liken the state to love. In essence, love is surrender. Love is a submission. It is putting others before yourself. A person who is filled with love may even give up his or her life for a beloved or to a cause. What draws us to these higher planes is a divine manifestation of love. It is like a billion-watt bulb. The love is so great that we merge with our beloved. We merge with the infinite.

Some describe this ultimate entry into the final level as a second death. A point comes when you will leave the levels of the afterlife that have form and move forward into the causal planes. There is a demarcation between these two states because it requires a major impetus of the soul to move to the next plane. You surrender your self-importance and your ego once and for all. You allow your own free will to merge with God's will. The lower self dies, and the higher self is set free. It is definitely like a death and a new birth.

The spirit communications made by Myers to the members of the Society for Psychical Research tell of seven deaths before the highest level is reached. Myers communicants assert that we are housed in a sequence of bodies. The bodies in the life beyond are made of a lighter and more highly energized substance than the physical body, with an increasing content of spiritual energy as we progress. Each entry into a higher level of the afterlife calls for spiritual preparation for the move to the next stage. Stage one is the earth plane and stage two is the earth-like world that we encounter immediately after death. Myers calls this simply the *life-immediately-after-death plane*. Also existing are five other planes which he calls *Hades,* the *world of Eidos* (plane of color), the *world of Helios* (plane of spiritual flame), and the final two planes, which he calls the *plane of light* and *timelessness*. These final two planes are akin to the causal planes.

In the causal planes, personality becomes of little importance even though your sense of self continues. You will be in a state similar to an artist lost in his inspiration, or lovers lost in a moment of joy. In fact, nothing is really lost. Everything that constitutes "you" is still there, including all of your personal memories and the history of your many lifetimes. It is a little like putting sugar into water. The sugar dissolves, but it is still there—you can taste it. Similarly, you will merge with these higher planes, and all that is you will still exist, but in a transformed state.

Spiritual beings from the causal planes can continue to manifest self and may descend to other levels in order to teach and help others up the ladder of spirituality. These beings are the higher guides, the angels, the avatars, and bodhisattvas.

As with all levels of the afterlife, there are still different states of being created by different types of people. Many will feel the impulse to return to teach others, whereas others may be so enchanted by the glorious light of God that they spend their time in a blissful state of rapture. They say that if you listen very carefully during your meditations, you may hear the angels singing.

Attuning to the Causal Worlds

You may feel that the states of being I have described here are very remote. They are beyond this earthly life and beyond the afterlife. How can we possibly understand them, and what relevance can they be to our life here and now?

The truth is that, even on this earthly plane, we can occasionally have a glimpse of the higher states of existence. Often, these experiences happen at a time of great emotional or spiritual tension, but they can also spring up suddenly, without any discernible reason.

Could it be that, at such times, you are somehow linked by a mystical thread to the causal world? Even the highest of the highest is reflected in every atom of this world.

This experience cannot be induced but rises spontaneously. However, sometimes a scene of great beauty or a magnificent piece of music can momentarily link you with such an overwhelming surge of feeling. Here is a short meditation that may help you to understand a bit about what this oceanic experience is like. Read it through, then lie down and contemplate these ideas. Perhaps you will be lucky and have a momentary glimpse of the beyond.

Meditation Exercise: The Oceanic Experience
Let yourself relax, and allow your mind to float free. You no longer need to worry about the troubles of your life, or the everyday thoughts that normally hold your attention. Spend a little time allowing your breathing to quiet and the tensions and worries to fall away from you.

Let peace surround you and fill you.

Now imagine that you are bathed in a brilliant pure white light. The light is so stupendous that all the myriad events of your life are insignificant in comparison. Your job, your skills, your relationships, your family—all are irrelevant when measured against this ineffable state. Here, as you reach further, these daily activities are not meaningless but give added value from the realization of their transience. Nothing can compare to this moment of revelation. You are touching a higher level of being.

For a short moment, you experience a wave of feeling, when everything you are seems insignificant. For a split second, you have a wordless awareness that everything is perfect. There is nothing in the universe to worry about. Everything is as it should be. Can you feel the cosmic flow of the life force running like a river of peace through everything that is? Behind the clatter of the world you may sense a world of silence. You come from nowhere and are going nowhere. Experience the oneness of everything. All is timeless. You are at one with the past, present, and future. The "I" with which you are familiar is not the real "I." All is One.

When you have spent some time with these thoughts, return to your normal consciousness and think about the feelings and thoughts this short meditation triggered within you.

Naturally, it is not possible to induce the preternatural sense of the divine. These things come spontaneously, often when we least expect them. However, a simple meditation like this can help to open you to the potential of the experience, and possibly allow you to flow with it should the opportunity for higher awareness be given you. It's an experience that reveals that the material world is not all there is. The sudden flash of true consciousness reminds us of the eternal planes that are our true home.

WE ARE IN HEAVEN NOW

"You can't die for the life of you."

—Doris Stokes

❧

I HAVE SPOKEN ABOUT HOW the afterlife consists of many planes of being and that the world around us manifests according to the inner state of the soul. Although it is not as apparent, this world that we live in now is very similar.

We assume that the objective world is a reality. It is something that can be measured and explained by science. But what becomes of the objective world when a holy man materializes an object or something is apported at a séance? Even mental mediumship defies the rules of the objective world. The truth is that even in this material world there are many planes of existence. The objective world is just one of these states. It is a plane where we all agree that the universe is the way it is. Our agreement makes it so.

The "laws" of the objective world say that I cannot be in two places at once. So why is it that some of us can use remote viewing to see places far away without using the five senses? The "laws" of the objective world say that time travels in a straight line. So why is it that some of us have precognition of the future or retrocognition of the past? The "laws" of the objective world say that the brain generates awareness. So why is it that some people can travel out of their body? The "laws" of the objective world say that matter cannot be created out of nothingness. So how can an object materialize at a séance or a spoon be bent by the mind?

It is not surprising that many scientists reject all of these phenomena. It would overturn their cherished belief in a mechanical, objective universe.

The mystic's answer to these questions is to say that the external world is an illusion. The true reality is not what lies outside us but what lies within. As our inner world changes, so we begin to see the outer world in a different way. We may become aware of spiritual energies around living things; thoughts shared between people; and the strange coincidences that happen when we embark on a spiritual path. We begin to understand that even the material world is molded by our consciousness. There is no objective reality.

Mysticism also teaches that "All is One." Everything has its being and is sustained by the universal energy that some call God. All planes of reality are different manifestations of God's nature. We, too, are God and can become aware of our divine nature. And just like God, we are omnipresent.

The laws that govern the spiritual worlds also govern this world. The way you think and act changes the circumstances around you, attracting good or bad fortune. What happens in one place affects what happens in another. For example, if you think well of someone who is far away, they will respond to your thoughts. Absent healing works in this way.

If you let your attention become centered inwardly, you will begin to perceive the world in a new way. In the first place, you will become less disappointed, for you will realize that all things are subject to change and cannot give you solace. Being so centered, you will also see that your happiness is your natural state of consciousness, when the mind is not distracted by material desires.

In the afterlife, the world around you is generated by your inner consciousness. Here, it is easier to understand that happiness springs from within. The same rule applies to this world. The events that happen to you are caused by your own actions and thoughts. They arise from experiences gained in this life and lives you have lived before. You bring it all upon yourself.

You may see and experience many beautiful new things when you enter the afterlife. However, heaven is familiar to you and will not feel like an alien world. This is because the fundamental things that constitute "you" remain the same. You continue to use perceptions, you continue to see an objective world, and you retain memory, character, and your personality. What differs is the fact that the environment around you is malleable and influenced by your thoughts. As you enter different levels of consciousness, your world reacts accordingly.

The laws that govern the earth are the same as those that govern the afterlife. In the life beyond, thought creates the world in an instant. Here on earth, the vibrations are slower, so it takes a little longer for consciousness to instigate change. Nonetheless, both worlds are a result of your inner life, which exists in all worlds simultaneously. Heaven is not somewhere different. It is here, alive inside you. In your heart, your loved ones are speaking to you right now to tell you about their joy of knowing the bliss of eternity. Can you feel them close to you? Can you feel their love echoing in your heart? Part of you lives with them and knows that there is nothing to fear in death. Everything is you. Everything is as it should be. Everything is good.

NOTES

Page iii: Henry Scott Holland (1847–1918), Canon of St. Paul's Cathedral, London.

Page 9: Ramakrishna quote. From *Graceful Exits* by Sushila Blackman. Source unknown.

Page 19: Yogananda quote. From *The Life beyond Death* by Arthur Ford, ABACUS, 1974, page 151, and from *Autobiography of a Yogi,* by Paramahansa Yogananda, Self Realization Publishers, copyright 1979, first published 1946, page 476.

Page 20: Lindbergh quote. From *The Spirit of St. Louis,* by Charles A. Lindberg, Charles Scribner's Sons, New York, 1953.

Page 28: Sathya Sai Baba quote. From *Gems of Wisdom,* by Sathya Sai Baba, Sathya Sai Publications, Trust India, page 34.

Page 30: Whitman quote. From *Encyclopaedia of Spirituality,* by Timothy Freke, Godsfield Books, 2000.

Page 31: From *The Psychic Casebook,* by Craig Hamilton-Parker, Sterling Publishing, New York.

Page 39: Edwards quote. From *Life in Spirit,* by Harry Edwards, Psychic Press Ltd., London, 1976.

Page 42: Greenfield quote. From *Brain Story,* by Susan Greenfield, BBC Worldwide Ltd., London, 2000.

Page 62: Jung quote. From *Encyclopaedia of Spirituality,* by Timothy Freke, Godsfield Books, 2000.

Page 64: Jung quote. From *On Dreams and Death,* by Marie-Louise von Franz, Shambhala, 1987, page 156.

Page 67: Ram Dass quote. From *Still Here,* by Ram Dass, Hodder and Stoughton, London, 2000.

Page 68: Kenneth Ring account. From *The After Death Experience,* by Ian Wilson, Corgi edition, Morrow, New York, 1989, page 140.

Page 71: From *Dying to Live,* by Susan Blackmore, 1993, Grafton (Harper Collins).

Page 74: Qur'an quote: From *The Koran,* (Oxford University Press), chapter 55, verse 26, as interpreted by Arthur Arberry.

Page 75: Gallagher account. From *Heading toward Omega,* by Kenneth Ring, pages 39, 40; also *The After Death Experience,* by Ian Wilson (op. cit.), page 174.

Page 79: Moody account. From *Life after Life,* by Raymond Moody, Bantam Books, page 76.

Page 82: Swedenborg quote. From *Compendium of the Theological and Spiritual Writings of Emanuel Swedenborg.*

Page 86: Sathya Sai Baba quote. From *Gems of Wisdom,* by Sathya Sai Baba (op. cit.), page 80.

Page 87: Jung quote. From *Memories, Dreams, Reflections,* by Carl Jung.

Page 87: Jung quote. From *Jung for Beginners,* Icon Books.

Page 95: Ford quote. From *The Life beyond Death,* by Arthur Ford (op. cit.).

Page 98: Silver Birch quote. From *Philosophy of Silver Birch*, edited by Stella Storm, Psychic Press, London, 1969, page 154.

Page 100: Fleites quote. From *Signals,* by Joel Rothschild, New World Library, Novato, California, 2000.

Page 103: Da Vinci quote. From *Design for Dying,* by Timothy Leary, Harper Collins, New York, 1997, page 131.

Page 105: From *Life in the World Unseen,* by Anthony Borgia, Odhams Press Limited, London. (First published by Psychic Press Ltd., London, 1988.)

Page 106: From *Life in Spirit,* by Harry Edwards, The Healer Publishing Co., Guildford, Surrey, 1976.

Page 106: From *Reaching to Heaven,* by James Van Praagh, Piatkus Books, London; also Dutton/Penguin, 1999.

Page 108: Cowan account. From *Reincarnation,* by Roy Stemman, Piatkus Books, London, culled from Sai Baba books.

Page 109: From *Memories, Dreams, Reflections,* by Carl Jung, first published by Collins and Routledge Paul, London, 1963.

Page 114: Swedenborg account. From *Heaven and Hell,* by Emanuel Swedenborg, translated from the Latin. Published by The Swedenborg Society, London, 1922, page 389 (originally published circa 1746).

Page 116: Findlay account. From *The Unfolding Universe,* by Arthur Findlay, Headquarters Publishing Co., London, 1935, page 270.

Page 116: Lodge account. From *Raymond,* by Sir Oliver Lodge. Quote from *The Life beyond Death,* by Arthur Ford (op. cit.).

Page 118: J. R. R. Tolkien quote. From *The Hobbit,* by J. R. R. Tolkien (1892–1973).

Page 125: Moen quote. From *Voyages into the Afterlife* (vol. 3), by Bruce Moen, Hampton Roads Publishing, Charlottesville, Canada, page 248.

Page 127 Aleksandrov quote. From *The Home Planet,* by Kevin W. Kelly and Jacques Cousteau, Addison Wesley, 1988.

Page 131: Swedenborg account. From *Heaven and Hell,* by Swedenborg (op. cit.), page 165.

Page 132: Edwards account. From *Life in Spirit,* by Harry Edwards, Harry Edwards Spiritual Healing Trust, Guilford, UK, 1976.

Page 133: Moody account. From *Afterlife,* by Colin Wilson, Grafton, Glasgow, 1998; quoting from Raymond A. Moody, *Reflections on Life After Life,* Corgi Books, London, 1977.

Page 134: Plutarch quote. *Life of Timoleon,* by Plutarch, written 75 A.C.E., translated by John Dryden.

Page 136: Myers account. From *Raymond,* by Sir Oliver Lodge, and from *The Life beyond Death,* by Arthur Ford (op cit), page 108.

Page 137: Myers quote: From *The Life beyond Death,* by Arthur Ford (op. cit.), page 109.

Page 138: Findlay quote. From *The Unfolding Universe,* by Arthur Findlay, Psychic Press Ltd., London, 1935, page 271.

Page 140: Kirmond quote. From *Messages from Heaven,* by Patricia Kirmond, Summit University Press, Corwin Springs, Montana, 1999, page 101.

Page 148: Zukav quote: From *The Seat of the Soul,* by Gary Zukav, Rider, London, 1990, page 207.

Page 150: Silver Birch quote. From *Philosophy of Silver Birch*, edited by Stella Storm (op. cit.).

Page 157: Milton quote. From *Paradise Lost: The First Book,* by John Milton, 1667.

Page 162: From *A Lawyer Presents a Case for the Afterlife—Irrefutable Objective Evidence,* by Victor Zammit, Krylov, Russia, 2007.

Page 168: Wickland account. From *Thirty Years among the Dead,* by Carl A. Wickland, Spiritualist Press, London, 1924, page 128.

Page 176: Rossetti quote. From *Original Text: Poems: An Offering to Lancashire, 1863. Dante Gabriel Rossetti, Poems*, Ellis and White, London, 1881, Fisher Rare Book Library, Toronto.

Page 177: From *Journey of Souls,* by Michael Newton, Ph.D., Llewellyn Publications, St. Paul, Minnesota, 1996, page 122.

Page 181: Blake quote. From "Poems from the Notebook," 1791–2.

Page 184: Frost quote. From "Stopping by the Woods on a Snowy Evening," original text by Robert Frost, *New Hampshire: A Poem with Notes and Grace Notes*, Henry Holt and Co., New York, 1923, p. 87. Fisher Rare Book Library, Toronto.

Page 192: Stokes quote. From *Joyful Voices,* by Doris Stokes, Futura, London, 1987.

INDEX